Men-at-Arms • 501

Armies of the Greek-Turkish War 1919–22

Philip S. Jowett • Illustrated by Stephen Walsh

Series editor Martin Windrow

First published in Great Britain in 2015 by Osprey Publishing
PO Box 883, Oxford, OX1 9PL, UK
PO Box 3985, New York, NY 10185–3985, USA
E-mail: info@ospreypublishing.com

Osprey Publishing, part of Bloomsbury Publishing Plc

A CIP catalogue record for this book is available from the British Library

Print ISBN: 978 1 4728 0684 0
PDF ebook ISBN: 978 1 4728 0685 7
ePub ebook ISBN: 978 1-4728 0686 4

Editor: Martin Windrow
Index by Rob Munro
Typeset in Helvetica Neue and ITC New Baskkerville
Originated by PDQ Media, Bungay, UK
Printed in China through Worldprint Ltd

15 16 17 18 19 10 9 8 7 6 5 4 3 2 1

Osprey Publishing is supporting the Woodland Trust, the UK's leading woodland conservation charity, by funding the dedication of trees.

www.ospreypublishing.com

Dedication

To my family

Acknowledgements

My thanks to the following contributors: Bulent Nuri Tutunc Uoglu, Chris Flaherty, Nikos Panos, Nejdat Turk, the Turkish Air Force Archives, the staff of the Greek Army Archives, and Paul Walsh.

Artist's Note

Readers may care to note that the original paintings from which the colour plates in this book were prepared are available for private sale. All reproduction copyright whatsoever is retained by the Publishers. All enquiries should be addressed to:

http.//www.stephenwalshillustrations.co.uk

The Publishers regret that they can enter into no correspondence upon this matter.

OPPOSITE Mustafa Kemal Pasha, the renowned commander of the 19th Division and later *de facto* field commander of the whole Ottoman force at Gallipoli in 1915. Untainted by close association with the 'Young Turks' regime led by Enver Pasha, upon the capitulation of the Ottoman Empire in 1918 he began planning armed resistance to the Allied and Greek occupation of Anatolia. After leading his Nationalist Army to final victory over the Greeks in 1922 he went on to rule as president of the new Turkish Republic until his death in 1938, being known from 1934 as Atatürk, 'Father of the Turks'. Here he wears his characteristic black lambswool *kalpak* hat, and the gold-on-red collar insignia with laurel and palm edging of *musir* (field marshal) that was personal to him. During the Greek-Turkish War he seldom wore rank badges, claiming that the sultan's government in Constantinople had dismissed him from the army.

ARMIES OF THE GREEK-TURKISH WAR 1919–1922

INTRODUCTION

The war fought from 1919 to 1922 between the Greeks and Turks in Anatolia – the region known to Greeks since Classical times as Asia Minor – was a direct result of the break-up of the defeated Ottoman Empire in 1918. Described here for simplicity as the Greek-Turkish War, it began with the invasion of Anatolia by the Greek Army in May 1919, and ended with their defeat by the Turkish Nationalists in September 1922. In Greece the war is usually called the Asia Minor Campaign, or – because of its eventually disastrous outcome – the 'Great Catastrophe'. In Turkey it is always known as the War of Independence, because the result of the Nationalist victory was the emergence of the modern Turkish Republic from the ruins of the Ottoman Empire.

The Ottoman Empire's decision to join the Central Powers (Germany and Austro-Hungary) in November 1914 had led to political and military disaster for the Turks, whose defeat in 1918 saw the loss of most of their former territories in the Middle East and Arabia. Under the terms of its armistice with the Entente (Allied) powers, the Empire was reduced to Anatolia in Asia Minor and Eastern Thrace on the tip of south-eastern Europe, with the new Sultan Mehmet VI being reduced to little more than a puppet of the Allies.

In June 1917 the neutralist King Constantine of Greece had been obliged to abdicate by the pro-Entente Prime Minister Eleftherios Venizelos. The latter declared war on the Central Powers, and actively joined the Entente campaign on the Salonika front which he had long supported. Despite factional disunity Greece put seven divisions into the field, fighting effectively against the Bulgarians in Macedonia. By the end of 1918 the Ottoman capital Constantinople and its surrounding Straits region were occupied by 50,000 British, French and Greek troops, and in southern and south-western Anatolia large regions were to be occupied by the French and Italians.

Although the Allies were unwilling to commit their own troops to occupation duties in Asia Minor, in their eyes the defeated Turks still needed to be punished. Accordingly, Britain, France, Italy and the USA encouraged the Greek government to invade western Anatolia and take control up to the designated 'Milne Line'. This would leave the Turks with only a rump state consisting of northern and eastern Anatolia.

The Turks could not be expected to accept these conditions; the 'Sentinel Association' began to plan resistance to any occupation forces, and a clandestine movement was formed under the leadership of Turkey's war hero of the Gallipoli campaign, Gen Mustafa Kemal. When the first Greek troops landed at the port of Smyrna (Izmir) in May 1919 only limited armed resistance was at first mounted by local irregulars, but amid episodes of savagery this quickly spread, as ethnic Greek communities profited from the Greek Army's penetration inland. Within a year, despite great difficulties, the creation of a new Turkish Nationalist Army was under way in defiance of the Allies and the nominal Caliphate government. Over the next two-and-a-half years the Greeks, Turkish Nationalists and other forces fought for control of Anatolia, and victory for the Nationalists in September 1922 led to the formation of the Turkish Republic. The struggle was accompanied by widespread atrocities against civilians on both sides, which it is not the purpose of this book to describe or to attempt to judge.

Ethnic make-up of the Anatolian population

Anatolia, the vast territory that now makes up the bulk of the Turkish Republic, was populated in 1919 by a mixture of various peoples whose ancestors had coexisted for many centuries. Christian Greeks had long lived within the Ottoman Empire, for the most part peacefully, side by side with Turks and other Muslim peoples, and spoke the same language. Although they had always maintained their separate identity and religion, they had little in common with their fellow Christians on the Greek mainland. In the 19th and early 20th centuries the population of Anatolia had been joined by Muslim refugees from Europe. These included Circassians driven out of the Caucasus by the Russians in the mid-19th century, and Albanians, and Pomaks or Bulgarian Muslims, who were both victims of the Balkan Wars of 1912–13. Other Muslim peoples in Anatolia included the Lazes of the Black Sea coastal region, the Kurds of the eastern provinces, and Arabs in the southern provinces. In addition there was a large Christian Armenian population, which was subjected to massacres during Ottoman persecutions from 1915 onwards.

Under the pressures of the Balkan Wars and World War I the previously uneasy but workable coexistence between these disparate communities proved fragile. When the Greek Army landed at Smyrna in 1919 many Anatolians took up arms to fight them, while many of their ethnic Greek and Armenian neighbours chose to fight alongside the invaders. This break-up of the Anatolian population into sharply defined religious camps would lead to cruel 'ethnic cleansing' by both sides, usually initiated by local forces but also carried out by regular troops. This reached its culmination in internationally recognized relocations of at least 1.75 million people in 1922–23, forever changing the face of what became modern Turkey.

CHRONOLOGY

1918

January–October   The Ottoman Empire, under the political leadership of the 'Young Turks' (war minister Enver Pasha, backed by Talaat Pasha, Djemal Pasha and Djavid Bey), faces defeat. As the wartime leadership flees Constantinople the remaining politicians seek to make peace with the Entente powers.

3 July: Mehmed VI is proclaimed the Turkish sultan and caliph (holding temporal and religious authority, respectively) after the death of Mehmed V.

30 October: The 'Mudros Armistice', signed between Ottoman successor government of Ahmed Izzet Pasha and Great Britain, ends Turkey's participation in World War I; Ottoman Army is limited to poorly equipped skeleton force of 50,000 men. Arabia, Syria, Palestine, and Mesopotamia are lost to the Ottoman Empire, and Armenia and Kurdistan are supposed to achieve independence. Entente powers reserve the right to occupy any part of remaining Ottoman territory that they deem threatens their security.

13 November: Warships of Entente navies sail into Constantinople.

1919

15 May: First of 12,000-strong Greek Army expeditionary force land at Smyrna, with the political support of the Entente powers and under the guns of the Entente navies.

19 May: Mustafa Kemal lands at port of Samsun under orders from the sultan's government in Constantinople to oversee the disbandment of Ottoman forces, but secretly begins planning resistance to Greeks.

21 June: Kemal and his supporters issue declaration of independence and summon Nationalist congress at Sivas.

4–13 September: Sivas congress establishes Representative Committee to govern Nationalist-held territory.

10 October: Entente forces take over Western Thrace (under Bulgarian control since 1913).

27 December: Turkish Nationalists establish capital at Ankara in Central Anatolia.

1920

January: French begin operations against Nationalists in Cilicia, carried out largely by their 10,000-strong Armenian Legion backed by colonial troops.

23 April: Turkish Grand National Assembly formed at Ankara.

Turkish soldiers in a hastily dug trench fire at the advancing Greeks; the man in the foreground is armed with a Russian Mosin-Nagant M1891 rifle. Their clothing appears to be a mixture of civilian and military items, with overcoats worn with soft hats and turbans. Their desperate shortage of all kinds of supplies obliged the Nationalist Army to use any type of available paramilitary clothing.

RIGHT Greek infantry pause on their long march through Anatolia to fill water bottles from a river. The soldiers wear a mixture of Adrian steel helmets (unpopular in the searing summer heat) and M1908 field caps with sun curtains; some have British Army surplus M1908 water bottles, while others fill up their metal mugs.

20 May:	Greece annexes Western Thrace.
22 June:	Greeks begin general advance in Anatolia.
12 July:	Greek Army moves into Eastern Thrace and establishes HQ at Adrianople; Turkish troops withdraw into Bulgaria (**31st**), but guerrilla resistance continues.
August:	Greek army in Asia Minor reaches 'Milne Line', where it will pause until early 1921 apart from local probes. Treaty of Sèvres (**10th**) signed by the sultan's government cedes Eastern Thrace, and Smyrna with surrounding territory, to the Greeks. It also agrees to the internationalization of the Straits and Constantinople, and allows Britain, France and Italy to establish 'zones of influence' in Turkish-controlled Anatolia. This highly unpopular agreement guarantees increased support for Mustafa Kemal and the Nationalists.
24 September–2 December:	**Turkish-Armenian War**, fought between 40,000-strong but poorly armed Army of Democratic Republic of Armenia, and 19,700-strong Nationalist Army of the East; the latter includes strongest remaining Ottoman Army formation, XV Corps under command of Kazim Karabakir, with 12,000 men and 40 guns. Nationalists' victory secures their eastern frontier, and releases large numbers of troops for coming campaigns against the Greeks.
September–October:	In Western Anatolia, Turks abandon linear defence and trade ground for time, denying Greeks opportunities for decisive engagements.
25 October:	King Alexander of Greece dies from blood poisoning (the result of a monkey bite received in his palace grounds).
14 November:	Greek Prime Minister Venizelos loses election to the monarchist 'United Opposition', and Dimitrios Gounaris forms government.

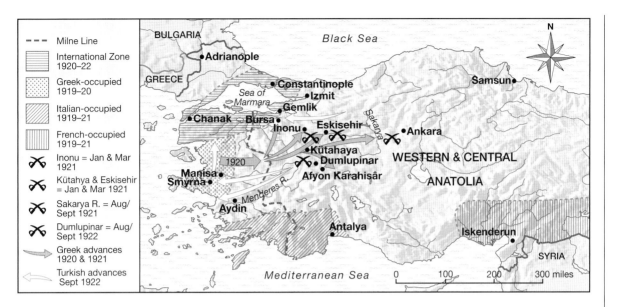

Legend:
- – – – Milne Line
- International Zone 1920–22
- Greek-occupied 1919–20
- Italian-occupied 1919–21
- French-occupied 1919–21
- ✗ Inonu = Jan & Mar 1921
- ✗ Kütahya & Eskisehir = Jan & Mar 1921
- ✗ Sakarya R. = Aug/Sept 1921
- ✗ Dumlupinar = Aug/Sept 1922
- ➡ Greek advances 1920 & 1921
- ⬅ Turkish advances Sept 1922

BULGARIA • Adrianople
GREECE
Black Sea
N
Sea of Marmara
Constantinople • Izmit
• Chanak • Bursa • Gemlik
Inonu • Eskisehir
Sakarya
• Ankara
• Kütahaya
• Dumlupinar
WESTERN & CENTRAL
Manisa • 1920 • Afyon Karahisâr
Smyrna •
ANATOLIA
Menderes R.
Aydin •
Antalya •
Samsun •
Iskenderun •
SYRIA
Mediterranean Sea   0   100   200   300 miles

5 December: Greek popular plebiscite votes to return the late King Alexander's father, the exiled King Constantine, to the throne. He is distrusted by the Allied powers because of his hostile stance in World War I; in future they will reduce aid to the Greek Army, and each will pursue its own clandestine diplomatic agenda. King Constantine announces his intention to participate actively in the military campaign in Asia Minor, and purges the army command.

1921

6–10 January: Greek probe towards Ankara is repulsed by Turks at **first battle of Inonu**, half way between Constantinople and Ankara, where 6,000 Nationalists hold back 18,000 Greeks joined by 4,650 Circassian rebels.

March: Reinforced Greek offensive towards Ankara. In return for handover of Batum to the Bolsheviks, Treaty of Friendship is signed between Nationalists and embryo Soviet Union, provoked by Entente powers' interventions in Civil War on behalf of White armies. This pact will greatly ease Nationalists' shortage of weapons.

28–30 March, second battle of Inonu: 15,000 Nationalists commanded by Ismet Pasha again make a stand, though outnumbered 2:1. In the first real test of the newly organized Turkish regular forces the Greek advance is checked, and withdraws to its original positions.

Basic sketch map of the theatre of war, 1919–22.

These Nationalist soldiers photographed outside their headquarters wear uniforms in the wide variety of khaki shades typical of Turkish troops during the war. Many wear the new cylindrical soft military hat in various heights and shapes, with star-and-crescent badges sewn on or stitched directly onto the fabric. Some officers in the left background and right foreground wear the *kalpak*, the most popular type of officers' headgear during the early years of the conflict. Note that several of the soldiers have German stick-grenades hanging from their leather bandoliers.

Colonel Nikolaos Plastiras, the heroic commander of the 5/42nd Evzone Regt, whose men fought with distinction in Asia Minor from 1919. Evzone regiments, which had two battalions each of four companies, were given dual designations: this unit was thus simultaneously the 5th Evzone Regt and 42nd Inf Regiment. Plastiras was known as the 'Black Rider' by the Greeks, but the Turks nicknamed his troops *Seytan Asker*, 'Satan's Soldiers'. When the Greeks were retreating in September 1922 Plastiras's men, detached from 13th Div to serve as I Corps reserve troops, were one of the few units to keep their discipline to the end. In this wartime photo the colonel wears standard officers' uniform, with the five black cord bands around his képi that identify his rank. On his left sleeve he has ten inverted chevrons, showing that he has served in the front lines in World War I and Asia Minor for a total of five years.

June: Captured Greek and Armenian irregular commanders are executed by the Nationalists. As part of their suppression campaign they force-march some 35,000 Anatolian Greek men into the desert, where most die.

July: Greek Army C-in-C LtGen Leonidas Paraskeropoulos leads well-organized summer offensive with 126,000 men, 410 artillery pieces, 4,000 machine guns and 20 aircraft. Facing them are 122,000 Turks with 160 guns, 700 machine guns and 4 aircraft. Greek forces advance in a three-pronged attack which sweeps the defending Nationalist formations ahead of them.

Italian forces begin withdrawal from south-west Anatolia, by secret agreement with Nationalists.

10–24 July, battles of Kütahaya and Eskisehir: These Greek victories over a 55,000-strong Turkish army cost the Nationalists about 4,000 killed, 10,000 wounded and many deserters. Reduced to about 30,000, the field army is forced eastwards on the verge of defeat.

5 August: Mustafa Kemal named commander-in-chief of the Nationalist Army by Grand National Assembly in Ankara.

14 August: Greeks renew their summer offensive across Central Anatolia, but their advance is hampered by the desert heat, poor maps, overstretched supply lines, shortages of ammunition and food, and outbreaks of malaria.

23 August–13 September, battle of the Sakarya: In this three-week battle on the east bank of the Sakarya river some 60 miles west of Ankara, 123,700 Greeks with 386 guns and 18 aircraft are resisted by 101,700 Turks with 196 guns and 2 aircraft. It results in stalemate, but prompts King Constantine to order a Greek withdrawal westwards on 14 September, reaching the Eskisehir–Afyon Karahisâr line by the 23rd. Both armies suffer roughly equal battle casualties – about 4,000 dead and 18,000–19,000 wounded.

20 October: France signs secret Treaty of Ankara with the Turkish Nationalists, ending its operations in Cilicia and beginning withdrawal under agreed terms.

October–December: Both sides hold their positions while they spend the rest of the year recovering and reinforcing. The Turks recruit, train and equip a new army in preparation for 1922.

1922

January–May: The stand-off between the Greeks and the Nationalists continues throughout the spring, on a front of about 450 miles. This front stretches between Cius on the Sea of Marmara south-eastwards to a salient around Eskisehir, south to another around Afyon Karahisâr, west and south over the Akar Dag mountain massif,

	then follows the right bank of the Büyük Menderes river to the Aegean coast.
25 May:	Greek C-in-C Gen Papoulas resigns command of Army of Asia Minor and is replaced by Gen Georgios Hatzianestis. The new commander, who will be described as being of 'unsound mind', will prove unable to cope with the pressures of his appointment.
August:	The Greek Army's total strength is reportedly some 225,000 men, with armament including 3,139 light and 1,280 heavy machine guns and 418 artillery pieces. Some 140,000 men out of this total are stationed in Anatolia, but because of the huge demands of the rear areas only some 80,000 of them, with 348 guns, are in the front lines. The 450-mile front means ridiculous divisional frontages averaging 30–40 miles. Greek III Corps (LtGen Soumilas) are responsible for the northern sector down to and including the Eskisehir salient; I Corps (Lt Gen Trikoupis) cover the southern sector around the Afyon Karahisâr bulge, but two gaps each of several miles are left uncovered in this sector; II Corps (MajGen Digenis) are in general reserve, ready to support whichever corps is threatened; and south-westwards to the Aegean coast second-line troops guard the Büyük Menderes river. Command and control from GHQ in Smyrna is overstretched and unwieldy.

25 August–2 September, battle of Dumlupinar: With roughly equal strength in infantry and artillery, but a 4:1 advantage in cavalry, the Turks launch their 'Great Summer Offensive' along a 30-mile front. Second Army faces Greek III Corps in the northern sector, and reinforced First Army confronts Greek I Corps backed by II Corps in the south around Afyon Karahisâr.

Turkish cavalry penetrate I Corps' front **(night of 25/26th)** and cut telegraph and rail links to the rear. Second Army launch fixing attacks on Greek III Corps; First Army's IV and I Corps, preceded by very effective bombardments, hit Greek I Corps north-westwards, drawing in part of II Corps **(26th)**. Greek communications with Smyrna HQ, and between corps and divisions, break down; Turkish IV Corps break through Greek I Corps, which retreats **(27th)**. 1st and 7th Divs from I and II Corps (Frangou Group) and rest of I Corps (Trikoupis Group) fall back separately towards Dumlupinar, pressed hard by Turkish IV, I and II, V Cavalry and VI Corps **(28th)**; periodically outflanked by cavalry, units take heavy losses and some collapse. Increasingly disorganized, Trikoupis Group fights its way towards Frangou Group at Dumlupinar, but is encircled

(29th). With only about 7,000 effective combatants left out of 22,000 men, Trikoupis marches for Alören and Banaz, pursued on his flanks by Turkish VI, V Cavalry and IV Corps (30th); meanwhile Frangou Group around Dumlupinar, attacked by Turkish I Corps, tries to hold a path open for Trikoupis. After a stand near Alören, Trikoupis Group breaks up and survivors flee in three columns; Gen Trikoupis surrenders with the largest on **2 September**, when Turks also take Eskisehir from III Corps. The Greeks suffer some 35,000 killed and wounded and 15,000 taken prisoner; Turkish losses from 22 August to 9 September are reported as 13,476 killed and wounded, 1,697 missing and 101 captured.

1–9 September: Rapid Nationalist advances over 250 miles in northern and southern thrusts retake all territory lost since May 1919. In the south they capture Aydin and Manisa (**7th**), and in the north Gemlik and Mudanya, where a complete Greek division surrenders (**11th**). Turkish booty is variously reported as about 40,000 rifles, at least 2,000 machine guns, most of the Greek artillery, 1,400 motor vehicles and 11 aircraft. Greek troops pursue a 'scorched earth' policy as they retreat to various ports of Western Anatolia. The majority of Greek soldiers are evacuated by sea to Thrace and the islands of Lesbos and Chios.

9 September: Nationalist Army enters Smyrna, and a few days later the Greek and Armenian quarters of the city are burnt to the ground amid scenes of atrocity. These events are still bitterly disputed today: the Turks blamed Greek and Armenian arsonists, but were in turn blamed by the Greek government and by foreign observers. About 10,000 Greek and Armenian

A Turkish general photographed with a unit of Nationalist lancers on the outskirts of Smyrna in September 1922. The general has the three stars of his rank on the square collar patches of his otherwise plain tunic, while the more junior officers behind him have triangular patches; this system was not officially introduced until 1923, but had already been in use for a couple of years previously. The cavalrymen wear forms of the cylindrical soft hat by now worn by much of the Nationalist Army, and have black-over-red lance pennants.

civilians are reported to have been killed. In total some 213,000 Greeks, Armenians and others are evacuated from the port by Entente ships. The Greek government falls.

26 September: Second abdication of King Constantine of Greece.

(September, Chanak Crisis: Nationalist Army advances north towards positions held by Entente troops in the Constantinople region. Under threat of all-out war between the Turks and the Entente powers a compromise is reached, and the occupying forces begin to evacuate the capital.)

(August–October: On the European front, Nationalists push Greek Army out of Eastern Thrace.)

11 October: Armistice of Mudanya between Nationalists and British, French and Italians.

November: Turkish Grand National Assembly abolishes the Sultanate (**1st**). Eight Greek politicians and military commanders are tried for high treason for their role in the disaster in Asia Minor; six are executed (**28th**), including Gen Hatzianestis and former Prime Minister Gounaris.

1923

January: From the end of the fighting in late 1922, a forced relocation of populations takes place on a scale then unprecedented in modern times, amid terrible suffering and many deaths. In total, more than 1,250,000 Anatolian Greeks and other Christians are forcibly removed from or flee Turkish territory in Anatolia and Eastern Thrace. At the same time some 500,000 Muslims who had lived in the European provinces of the former Ottoman Empire for generations are relocated to the newly formed Turkish Republic.

24 July: Treaty of Lausanne recognizes these relocations, ends the Entente powers' occupation of Constantinople, and confirms their recognition of the Turkish Republic.

29 October: Mustafa Kemal becomes first president of the Republic.

War losses

Greek Army losses during the war were quoted officially as 19,362 battle dead plus 4,878 who died from disease and other causes, and 18,095 missing. They also admit 48,880 wounded, and 10,000 taken prisoner by the Nationalists. Turkish claims of the Greek losses were much higher, at 120,000–130,000 killed and wounded, and some historians agree on a figure of around 100,000. Turkish military losses were estimated at less than half those figures, although this too is probably a serious underestimate. (The chaos of events, incomplete archives, and continuing bitterness between Greece and Turkey all prevent an impartial resolution of such contradictions.)

Civilian deaths during the 'ethnic cleansing' that took place amongst both the Christian and the Muslim populations are even harder to determine, but were very numerous indeed. The mass abuse of minority communities within the Ottoman Empire had begun in 1915, and numbers before 1919 are difficult to separate out from the grand totals. During what was in some measure a bitter civil war in Anatolia in 1919–22, it was all too common for not only irregulars of both sides but also regular troops to destroy villages with great cruelty.

THE GREEK ARMY IN ASIA MINOR

By the 1918 Armistice the Greek Army had seven divisions on the Macedonian front (including I Army Corps with 1st, 2nd & 13th Divs, and II Army Corps with 3rd, 4th & 14th Divisions). The Asia Minor landing expedition of May 1919, initially known as the Army of Occupation (LtGen Nider) and led by the 1st Div, comprised I Corps (1st & 2nd Divs) and Smyrna Corps (13th and Archipelago Divs), totalling 12,000 men with 9,000 rifles, 18 heavy machine guns and 36 light machine guns. It was soon reinforced, and by the end of 1919 the retitled Army of Asia Minor (LtGen Miliotis-Komninos) had a strength of 2,400 officers and 57,028 enlisted men in the same four divisions plus the Smyrna Div in reserve.

In November 1920, following the monarchist restoration, LtGen Anastasios Papoulas took over command of the Army of Asia Minor, and some formations were redesignated for political reasons. In II Corps (previously 3rd and Cretan Divs) the Cretan Div was amalgamated with the Kydoniai Div to form the new 5th Division. The former Smyrna Army Corps became III Corps, with 7th (ex-Archipelago), 10th (ex-Smyrna) and 11th (ex-Magnesia) Divisions. By early 1921 the army had expanded to 3,972 officers and 103,545 enlisted men, and its armament included 297 artillery pieces of which 36 were heavy guns.

In March 1921 the Greeks called up three classes of reservists totalling 40,000 men, and later mobilized a further two classes; this

Greek troops advance into Western Anatolia after disembarking at Smyrna in May 1919; most have sun curtains on their M1908 field caps, as were also worn on the Greek sidecap. These soldiers were renowned for their resilience on the march, and could cover great distances in a day. Initially infantry regiments had two battalions each of three companies, and some bore names, e.g. early reinforcements that followed the 1st Div ashore included the 5th & 6th Archipelago and 8th Cretan Regiments. However, during the army purge following the restoration of King Constantine in late 1920 the names were discontinued for political reasons.

raised the size of the army to 200,000 men. They also began conscripting the local ethnic Greek population in Anatolia, who were often reluctant recruits. By summer 1922 it is reckoned that these latter may have represented up to 60,000 of the Greek Army's total strength of 225,000 men.

However, the virtual doubling in strength of the Greek Army during 1921 led to serious weaknesses, primarily because there were insufficient trained and competent officers to command the largely raw recruits who now flooded in. There was a bitter political schism between pro-monarchist and pro-Venizelos officers, and after King Constantine's return from exile in December 1920 a number of anti-monarchist officers were actually imprisoned and many others relegated to second-line roles. This left units under the command of pro-monarchist officers many of whom had not seen front-line service since 1913. Non-commissioned officers had to be promoted to fill the junior officer ranks; not only were many of these inadequately educated for their new role, but the loss of their experienced example was damaging to the rank-and-file. Junior officers who were promoted to fill field ranks in the expanded army often proved unequal to their new responsibilities, and the Army's morale was also undermined by a number of Communist officers who spread anti-war propaganda.

The rank-and-file of the Greek Army at the beginning of 1921 were made up largely of veterans of the fighting on the Salonika front in 1917–18, and others who had seen service with the Greek interventionist force in southern Russia in 1920. A British officer who inspected first-line Greek units in June 1921 described the army then as 'a more efficient fighting machine than I have ever seen it', but the subsequent rapid expansion led to these experienced veterans being outnumbered by new recruits from Greece and locally raised Anatolian conscripts. Some of the former were older men who had seen service in the Balkan Wars of 1912–13, war-weary after serving almost continuously since 1912, and many of the latter were very unwilling to leave their families and communities.

The Greeks also had difficulty organizing the army to operate in the punishing terrain of Anatolia. During the 1921 fighting the Greek supply system often broke down, with motor vehicles failing and draught animals dying. It was also plagued by poor communications between the overstretched units, with only one radio set per Army Corps, and the telegraph system being cut repeatedly by Nationalist irregular cavalry that roamed behind the lines. Greek cavalry units showed at a disadvantage against the Nationalists, being inferior in horses, arms and equipment; some troopers reportedly had to use Lebel bayonets for lack of sabres. Poor reconnaissance work by Greek cavalry and air units led to several critical mistakes by the high command during the war.

Five Greek gendarmes posing in the field during the Asia Minor campaign; the man in the centre displays the two white forearm stripes of a sergeant (see Plate C1). The winter woollen uniform is decorated with the white left shoulder cords of the Gendarmerie, dark blue collar tabs with silver buttons, and silver cap-badge crowns. Note the mounted troops' style of cartridge pouch with a button-down strap, here worn singly at the front of the belt, and the large haversacks and slung water bottles.

In this period postcard a Greek Evzone private poses proudly for the studio cameraman wearing the distinctive uniform of these elite mountain light infantry. He is wearing the *farizan* fez complete with its black tassel; his long *doulama* jacket covers the *fustinella* kilt, worn with a pair of thick white woollen stockings and *tsarouchia* shoes with pompons. The cartridge pouches on his belt appear to be German, and may be from stocks captured in Macedonia in 1917–18. He is armed with the Greek Army's standard Mannlicher-Schönauer M1903 rifle.

Greek, Armenian and Circassian irregulars

The military situation in Anatolia in 1919–22 was complicated by the presence of large numbers of irregulars fighting both for and against the Greeks. Many small, dispersed units of ethnic Greeks, Armenians and 'renegade' Circassians either fought for the Greek Army as auxiliary cavalry, or ranged the war zones in bands that both attacked Muslim towns and villages and defended their own against Turkish attacks. The Pontic Greek population from the southern shore of the Black Sea had been fighting the Turks since World War I; their 5,000 'Mauri Mira' or 'Black Fate' guerrillas defended their villages from Nationalist attacks, and in turn attacked Muslim villages. An additional 25,000 Pontic men and women described as 'armed sympathizers' were supplied by the Greek Army with limited numbers of rifles.

Circassians were split between pro-Nationalist and pro-Greek camps, although the great majority fought for the Nationalists. Those that did choose to join the Greek side usually did so to avoid incorporation under the regular Nationalist chain of command, but they could not truly be described as pro-Greek. One Circassian irregular leader went over to the Greeks taking with him 3,000 men, 4 field guns and 400 machine guns. Other smaller irregular bands, some with only 50–100 men, were drawn from the Muslim Pomak population originally from Bulgaria, and from Albanian refugees from the Balkan Wars of 1912–13.

REPRESENTATIVE ORDER OF BATTLE
Greek Army of Asia Minor, Battle of the Sakarya River, August 1921

C-in-C: LtGen Anastasios Papoulas
I Corps (MajGen Alexandros Kontoulis)
1st Division: 4th & 5th Inf Regts, 1/38th Evzone Regt
2nd Div: 1st, 7th & 34th Inf Regts
12th Div: 14th, 41st & 46th Inf Regts
Artillery Regt
II Corps (Prince Andrew)
5th Div: 33rd, 43rd & 44th Inf Regts
9th Div: 25th & 26th Inf Regts, 3/40th Evzone Regt
13th Div: 3rd & 2nd Inf Regts, 5/42nd Evzone Regt
Arty Regt
Army Reserve Heavy Arty Regt
III Corps (MajGen Giorgios Polymenakos)
3rd Div: 6th & 12th Inf Regts, 5/39th Evzone Regt
7th Div: 22nd, 23rd & 37th Inf Regts
10th Div: 27th, 28th & 30th Inf Regts
Arty Regt
16th Inf Regt (det from 11th Div)
Cavalry Brigade: 1st & 3rd Cav Regts
Southern Group of Divisions (MajGen Nikolaos Trikoupis)
4th Div: 8th, 11th & 35th Inf Regts
11th Div: 17th & 45th Inf Regts
9th, 49th, 18th & 47th Inf Regts

Circassian cavalry who have chosen to fight for the Greeks, pictured with a Greek officer in 1921; compare with Plate C3. They all wear lambswool *kalpaks* and have short overcoats partially covering their leather bandoliers and Caucasian daggers. They have probably brought their carbines with them; by this date the Greeks had few modern weapons to spare.

Greek Army, Battle of Dumlupinar, August 1922

C-in-C: LtGen Georgios Hatzianestis (HQ Smyrna)
Dispositions from north to south:
III Corps (MajGen Petros Soumilas, HQ Eskisehir)
11th Div; 3rd Div; 10th Div; Independent Div (Col Dimitrios Theotokis); *Eskisehir Command*
I Corps (MajGen Nikolaos Trikoupis, HQ Afyon Karahisâr)
5th Div; 12th Div; 4th Div; 1st Div plus 49th Inf Regt; *Plastiras Detachment* (Col Nikolaos Plastiras;
5/42nd Evzone Regt & 13th Mtn Arty Sqn) – det from 13th Div as I Corps reserve
II Corps (MajGen Kimon Digenis, HQ Gazligöl, NW of Afyon Karahisâr)
9th Div; 13th Div minus I Corps reserve units; *7th Div; Kütahaya Command* (4 bns); *2nd Div* reinforced,
covering southern flank of I Corps together with *Cavalry Div* under direct Army commmand.

Democratic Republic of Armenia, 1920

The army of the short-lived Armenian Republic, 1918–20, had an initial strength of 16,000 men with 800 officers, the latter almost exclusively veterans of service in the Russian Imperial Army before 1917. By 1919 it had grown to a total of 25,000–30,000 men, and by 1920, when it came into conflict with the Turkish Nationalist Army, it stood at 40,000. However, throughout its existence the Armenian Army struggled to obtain weapons and equipment. In 1918 it was disappointed when artillery promised by the British government was shipped instead to the White Russians. In 1920, as the Armenian Army faced defeat, Armenians in the country and abroad raised $1,250,000 to buy much-needed surplus British armaments. Only 60 per cent of the arms that were purchased with this money arrived in Armenia, and the shipments included no artillery.

TURKISH FORCES

The Turkish forces fighting the Greek Army from 1919 to 1922 were a mix of regular and irregular troops. For the first year of the war they were almost exclusively irregulars, although their leaders included a few ex-Ottoman Army officers. From 1920 onwards the formation of the regular Nationalist Army saw most of the effective irregular groups gradually absorbed into its ranks, and the rest disbanded.

A dark-complexioned Turkish irregular armed with a Mauser M1903 rifle poses with his horse during the fighting of 1919–20. Men like him were often virtual bandits who had hidden out in the Anatolian hills to avoid Ottoman military service, but when the Greeks invaded it was they who provided the backbone of the resistance until the Nationalist Army could be organized. Thereafter they often resisted coming under regular command, which was then imposed by force.

BELOW By contrast, a well-dressed and armed officer of the Turkish irregular forces poses in a studio. Possibly an ex-regular of the Ottoman Army, he wears a fleece *kalpak*, a lightweight tunic, woollen breeches and stockings and leather sandals, and has a pair of army binoculars. In addition to his Mauser rifle he has a German stick-grenade and a Luger P08 pistol on his right and left hips respectively. He carries plenty of ammunition in three leather waist bandoliers; these were usually worn like this, one above the other, each supported by a narrow strap over one shoulder.

The Ottoman Army, 1919

When the Greeks invaded Asia Minor in 1919 the remnants of the 560,000-strong Ottoman Army included a total of some 35,000 troops stationed in Thrace, the Straits region and Western Anatolia. Another 8,000 were in the Kurdish eastern region. The best-equipped and organized units were an additional 30,000 men of XV Corps (HQ Erzurum), which had been ordered back from Azerbaijan. Cilicia province in Southern Anatolia had another 18,000 troops, mainly of Syrian origin.

Turkish irregular forces – *Kuva-Yi Milliye*

When the Greek Army landed at Smyrna they faced little or no opposition from the Ottoman 'armistice' army, the only armed resistance coming from bands of patriotic irregulars often formed on an ad hoc basis by local leaders. 'Semi-political' brigands had always existed in the mountains of Western Anatolia, fighting against Ottoman gendarmes and local forces in the 19th and early 20th centuries. Although they kidnapped and robbed the locals they were usually careful to target the rich merchants and landowners, thus enjoying something of a 'Robin Hood' reputation among the rural poor. When the Ottoman Empire joined the Central Powers at the end of 1914 many of these men had avoided conscription into the Ottoman Army. Although such desperadoes owed no allegiance to any particular government, when the Greeks invaded Anatolia in 1919 they were more than prepared to fight them. Their estimated overall strength increased from about 5,000 in 1919 to 15,000 in 1920, by the absorption of ex-soldiers and other volunteers.

As well as these irregulars in Western Anatolia there were others fighting against the occupying French in the southern province of Cilicia and in Upper Mesopotamia. These were under the command of a number of regular army officers and were receiving instructions from Mustafa Kemal. Much of the bitterest fighting in Cilicia was against the large force of Armenian auxiliaries raised by the French Army.

When the nascent regular Nationalist Army tried to absorb these irregulars under their control they faced many problems. The irregulars were by nature independent-minded, and resisted placing themselves under the orders of regular officers. If a man joined the irregulars he could expect 'excellent equipment, a good horse, a silver-mounted whip and a belt of shining cartridges'. As well as his pay being up to three times that of a regular soldier, it usually arrived on time, and he could generally expect a much easier life. Irregulars were mobile troops who employed hit-and-run tactics, withdrawing from an unequal action so that they would live to fight another day. Regular troops, by contrast, were generally badly clothed and paid intermittently. They had to accept a rigid military discipline, being expected to make suicidal charges or to stand and fight to the death if necessary.

The female population of Anatolia were important to the Nationalist war effort in the support role. They worked in munitions factories and workshops, and were an important element of the army's supply system. A number of women even fought as irregulars in the bands that operated in Western and Southern Anatolia; some took up arms alongside their husbands in guerrilla groups, while others became famous for leading their own bands.

One of the most audacious women fighters was Kara Fatma (see Plate E2). She had previously fought in the Balkan Wars alongside her husband, and raised a small all-female unit on the Caucasus Front in World War I. After her husband was killed fighting the Armenians in 1920 she led a 35-strong volunteer band which included both her son and daughter, and fought in several actions during 1921–22. Captured by the Greek Army, she managed to escape, and at the end of the war she was awarded the honorary rank of second lieutenant in the Turkish Army. Another famous woman fighter was Rahime, known by the nickname of Tayyar or 'Flyer', who in 1920 joined an irregular band under Hussein Aga in Cilicia. She earned her fame largely by taking part in a raid on a French arms depot that netted 80 rifles and 2 machine guns, during which Rahime risked her life to bring back fallen comrades' bodies under fire for burial.

The Turkish Nationalist Army

The Turkish Nationalist Army that emerged in 1920 was a largely makeshift force created from the ruins of the Ottoman Army and including men from all elements of the diverse Muslim population of Anatolia. One commentator said that these included 'Sunni, Alevi, Turks, Kurds, Abaza, Tatars, Bosnians, Lazes, Pomaks and Arabs'. In 1919 the regular Nationalist Army had a reported strength of only 5,000 men, but by late 1920 it had expanded rapidly and boasted 86,515 all ranks.

In 1920 the initial 'divisions' could field only 2,500–3,000 men, and some were essentially battalions numbering only 300–700. In 1921 the organization of Nationalist divisions was standardized at 5,000 men made up of three infantry regiments with three battalions each. Each battalion was supposed to incorporate an artillery element when guns were available, and an elite assault or 'stormtrooper' element. The divisional establishment also had one company each of cavalry, engineers and medical troops. By 1922 the standard division was set at 9,000 men (though they averaged 7,500 in the field) with nine battalions and a 12-gun artillery regiment; by contrast, cavalry divisions had a strength of 3,000. By the time of their victorious 1922 summer offensive the Nationalist

Soldiers of the Turkish Nationalist Army parade for their leader Mustafa Kemal during the 1922 campaign. Their headgear is the new type of cylindrical soft hat based on those worn by Anatolian peasants, and made of various materials in various heights. Their smart uniforms are in Ottoman Army style, some worn with gaiters and others with puttees.

Army had reached a reported total strength of 207,940 men, armed with 100,530 rifles, 2,025 light and 835 heavy machine guns, and 323 artillery pieces of all types.

The Nationalist Army was not a totally cohesive force, and at times conscription had to be imposed to expand it; in an attempt to fill the ranks during the war the recruitment age limits were broadened to between 18 and 60 years. Although thousands of former irregulars joined the army during 1920–21, some joined (as one commentator put it) 'quietly, others by force'. Lack of regular pay was a major problem that led many commanding officers to petition the leadership in Ankara to try to improve matters. This was one of several factors that led to high rates of desertion during 1921 and into early 1922, but by the final offensive of summer 1922 most problems appear to have been solved, and an iron discipline was being enforced by Mustafa Kemal and his officers.

In March 1921 the Nationalist Army was organized into three Fronts. On the Eastern or Armenian Front the Third and Fifteenth 'Armies' totalled between 15,000 and 20,000 men. The Western Front was divided between Northern and Southern sectors; the former numbered around

This Nationalist soldier pictured at the end of the war is wearing the 'peakless képi' headgear, which was officially but retrospectively introduced under the 1923 regulations. Note the star-and-crescent badge; this was always in red cloth, but its background might be either khaki or green. The square, diagonally-quartered red-and-white badge on his left upper sleeve identifies him as a member of an Army HQ guard, which explains his relatively smart uniform; divisional HQ troops wore a red-over-white triangular pennant shape. His Ottoman Army brown leather equipment has the four German-type pouches with clips for his 7.65mm Turkish Mauser M1903 rifle.

REPRESENTATIVE ORDERS OF BATTLE
Turkish Nationalist Army, Battle of the Sakarya River, August 1921

C-in-C: MajGen Mustafa Kemal Pasha
CGS: Gen Mustafa Fevzi Pasha

Western Front (MajGen Ismet Pasha)
Cavalry Brigade: 21st Cav Regt, Adatepe Cav, Militia Inf
2nd Cav Div: 2nd, 4th & 13th Cav Regts
3rd Cav Div: 27th & 28th Cav Regts
Provisional Div: 35th & 52nd Inf Regts; 1st & 2nd Militia Regts
3rd Caucasian Div: 7th, 8th & 11th Inf Regts
6th Div: 34th, 50th & 51st Inf Regts; 17th–20th Stormtrooper Units
57th Div: 37th, 39th & 176th Inf Regts
29th & 47th–49th Inf Regts
Artillery Regt
Pioneer Bn

Provisional Group (Brig Kâzim 'Köprülü' Bey)
1st Cav Div: 10th, 11th & 14th Cav Regts
1st Div: 3rd, 4th & 5th Inf Regts
17th Div: 61st, 62nd & 63rd Inf Regts
41st Div: 12th, 16th & 19th Inf Regts
XII Group (Brig 'Deli' Halid Bey)
11th Div: 170th, 126th & 127th Inf Regts
IV Group (Brig Kemaleddin Sami Bey)
5th Caucasian Div: 9th, 10th & 13th Inf Regts
61st Div: 159th, 174th & 190th Inf Regts
III Group (MajGen Yusuf Izzet Pasha)
7th Div: 2nd, 23rd & 41st Inf Regts
8th Div: 131st, 135th & 189th Inf Regts
15th Div: 38th, 48th & 56th Inf Regts
II Group (Brig Selâhaddin Âdil Bey)
4th Div: 40th, 42nd & 58th Inf Regts
5th Div: 14th, 15th & 24th Inf Regts
9th Div: 25th, 26th & 27th Inf Regts
I Group (Brig Izzedin Bey)
23rd Div: 31st, 68th & 69th Inf Regts
24th Div: 30th, 31st & 32nd Inf Regts
V Cavalry Group (Brig Fahreddin Bey)
14th Cav Div: 3rd, 54th & 55th Cav Regts
4th Cav Div: 5th & 20th Cav Regts

Turkish Nationalist Army, Battle of Dumlupinar, August 1922

C-in-C: FM Mustafa Kemal Pasha
CGS: Gen Mustafa Fevzi Pasha

Western Front (MajGen Ismet Pasha)
Kocaeli Group det from Second Army (Brig 'Deli' Halid Bey)
18th Div: 15th & 24th Inf Regts
25th Hvy Arty Regt

First Army (MajGen Nureddin Pasha)
IV Corps (Brig Kemaleddin Sami Bey)
8th Div: 131st, 135th & 189th Inf Regts; Arty Regt
5th Caucasian Div: 9th, 10th & 13th Inf Regts; Arty Regt
11th Div: 70th, 126th & 127th Inf Regts; Arty Regt
12th Div: 34th, 35th & 36th Inf Regts; Arty Regt
I Corps (Brig Izzedin Bey)
23rd Div: 31st, 68th & 69th Regts; Arty Regt
15th Div: 38th, 45th & 56th Inf Regts; Arty Regt
14th Div: 25th, 26th & 30th Inf Regts; Arty Regt
57th Div: 37th, 39th & 176th Inf Regts; Arty Regt
V Cavalry Corps (MajGen Fahreddin Pasha)
1st Cav Div: 10th, 11th, 14th & 21st Cav Regts
2nd Cav Div: 2nd, 4th, 13th & 20th Cav Regts
14th Cav Div: 3rd, 5th, 34th & 54th Cav Regts
6th Div: 50th, 51st & 52nd Inf Regts; Arty Regt
Dina Detachment: 59th Inf Regt
II Corps (Brig Ali Hikmed Bey)
7th Div: 2nd, 23rd & 41st Inf Regts; Arty Regt
4th Div: 40th, 42nd & 58th Inf Regts; Arty Regt
3rd Caucasian Div: 7th, 8th & 11th Inf Regts; Arty Regt

Second Army (MajGen Yakub Shevki Pasha)
III Corps (Brig Shukri Naili Bey)
41st Div: 12th, 16th & 19th Inf Regts; Arty Regt
61st Div: 159th, 174th & 190th Inf Regts; Arty Regt
1st Div: 3rd, 4th & 5th Inf Regts; Arty Regt
Provisional Cav Div: 33rd, 37th & 38th Cav Regts
VI Corps (MajGen Kâzim Pasha)
16th Div: 43rd, 44th & 46th Inf Regts; Arty Regt
17th Div: 47th, 62nd & 63rd Inf Regts; Arty Regt
3rd Cav Div (Provisional): 27th & 28th Cav Regts

Cerkez Ethem, the controversial Nationalist commander whose Circassian 1st Mobile Force was deployed by Mustafa Kemal to subdue rebellions. His headdress, shirt, jacket and breeches are black, worn with either black or brown soft leather boots. Two bandoliers worn around the waist are supported by leather straps over the shoulders. He is armed with an ex-Greek Army Mannlicher-Schönauer M1907 carbine, a German Luger P08 pistol and a Circassian dagger.

13,000 men in the 1st, 4th, 11th, 24th and 61st Divs, and the latter some 11,000 men in the 8th, 23rd and 57th Divs plus the 12th, 14th and 18th Inf Bdes (which would subsequently form divisions with those numbers). On the Southern Front was the 17,000-strong Cilician XIII Corps, made up mainly of Syrian troops in the 2nd and 5th Divisions.

After the defeat of the Turks at the battles of Kütahaya and Eskisehir in July 1921 the Nationalist Army that fell back to the Sakarya river had dwindled from 70,000 to about 30,000 men, but its strength in the August–September battles is reported as three times that many, suggesting a truly extraordinary effort. Thereafter the army was rebuilt impressively during the lull before the next summer campaign. By mid-1922 it had been transformed, with intensive training especially in the use of artillery and cavalry. An officers' training school had been set up in Ankara in 1920, with its first graduates entering their units on 1 November that year. In 1922 the Greeks noticed a marked improvement in the performance of Turkish troops, down to such basic tactical skills as the digging of trenches and the sighting of machine guns. This led the Greek Army to insist that the Nationalists must be receiving foreign assistance, but in reality they had been able to retrain their army using only their own resources and the pool of experienced officers from the Ottoman Army.

Nationalist cavalry

Although the Ottoman cavalry had a good reputation pre-1918, there were never enough of them to make a great impact on the campaigns of 1914–18. During the Greek-Turkish War the role of the cavalry was vital, and their strength and mobility gave the Nationalist Army a distinct advantage. Mounted on sure-footed Anatolian hill ponies, they outflanked the Greek columns and raided behind their lines to great effect. When available, each trooper had two mounts so that he could swap over at intervals to increase the unit's range across country. On 1 September 1920 Gen Fevzi, the Nationalist Chief of Staff, ordered the creation of two cavalry divisions each having a strength of 3,000 men, and a school of horsemanship was also set up that year. As the Nationalist Army developed the cavalry arm was expanded; by early 1922 the V Cavalry Corps had three divisions, each of four regiments, totalling 10,450 men, with 48 machine guns and 16 field guns, which gave the Turks a decisive superiority over their opponents' single cavalry division. At the start of the 'Great Offensive' of summer 1922 the total number of Turkish cavalry had reached 12,000 men, of which nearly half would be committed in the battle of Dumlupinar.

Nationalist assault battalions

During the latter stages of World War I the Ottoman Army had established a number of 'stormtroop' assault units in Palestine and Transcaucasia. While the concept had proved successful in the armies of their German, Austro-Hungarian and Bulgarian allies, less is known about the Ottomans' employment of such units. When the Nationalist Army was formed it was soon decided to raise assault units on similar lines. Volunteers were chosen from amongst the ranks of the infantry divisions, favouring men with better physique and front-line experience; they were given better rations than the mass of the infantry, and the best of what weaponry and equipment were available. Some personnel may well have been veterans of the original Ottoman units who joined the Nationalists en bloc. A '1st Assault Bn' reportedly fought well at the battle of the Sakarya river, while suffering heavy losses (note that the order of battle on page 18 lists four numbered units, presumably of company size, within the 6th Division). Before the end of the war there was reportedly a company-sized assault unit in each infantry regiment, making up a battalion in each division.

The 1st Mobile Force – *Kuva-Yi Seyyare*

As the various irregular forces were absorbed into the regular Nationalist Army one group kept its separate identity. Entitled the 1st Mobile Force, this was led by the Circassian Cerkez Ethem. For a short period it acted

Tough-looking Kurdish fighters wearing traditional dress pose for the camera, armed with Mausers and festooned with bandoliers. It is impossible to tell from their appearance which side they are on; during the 1919–22 conflict the hard-pressed Nationalists faced several rebellions in Anatolia, including some by Kurdish tribes in the east.

as Mustafa Kemal's 'fire brigade', being rushed to put down rebellions against the Ankara government. At its peak the Mobile Force had a strength of 2,100 infantry and 1,300 cavalry, with a field gun, 4 mountain guns and 8 machine guns.

The Caliphate Army – *Kuva-Yi Inzibatiye*, 1920
The military forces available to the sultan's government in Constantinople from 1918 were limited both by Allied occupation of the city and by the lack of willing recruits; any who joined the sultan's ranks would be seen by the majority of Turks as traitors serving in a 'puppet' force. Besides a 300-strong Sultan's Guard other troops stationed in the capital guarded government buildings, but were not envisaged as having any wider military role. In 1920 the sultan was persuaded by the Allied powers to try to form a so-called Caliphate Army under Suleyman Selik Pasha, a former Ottoman commander. Raised in April 1920 and reaching a strength of 7,000 men, this was then sent against the Nationalist forces, but the campaign lasted only just over two months. When faced by the Nationalist Army the troops' morale soon collapsed, and after a heavy defeat the Caliphate Army was disbanded on 25 June, the great majority of its men then joining the Nationalists.

WEAPONS

Greek small arms
Many officers and senior NCOs retained handguns from the Balkan Wars of 1912–13 and Salonika campaigns of 1917–18. Older sidearms in service in 1919–22 included French St Etienne M1873 and M1874 revolvers, and semi-automatics included the Austro-Hungarian Mannlicher M1905, Mannlicher-Steyr, Browning M1903, and the Danish 9mm Bergmann-Bayard M1903.

The main rifle in service with Greek first-line troops was the Steyr-produced Mannlicher-Schönauer M1903 in 6.5mm. This effective weapon, which had a five-round rotary magazine loaded from stripper clips, had been in service with the Greek Army during the Balkan Wars, and a slightly modernized M1903/14 had been introduced in 1914 in rifle and carbine versions. If enough had been available it would have remained the only type in use, but the great expansion of the Greek Army in Asia Minor led to a demand for more rifles. The French 8mm Lebel M1886/93, and 10,000

LEFT Greek troops hunker down in a hilltop trench while under fire; all apart from the officer at the right wear Adrian steel helmets. At centre, note the French-supplied M1915 'Chauchat' LMG with its semi-circular magazines.

RIGHT Somewhere on the desolate plains of Anatolia, a Greek crew serve a French-supplied St Etienne M1907 machine gun. This obsolete weapon was issued to the Greek Army during its involvement in World War I in 1917–18, when it had to take whatever the Allies could spare. Note the contrasting shades of woollen and cotton uniform items.

This damaged photograph shows the Turkish Nationalist crews of four 'Chauchat' LMGs, with their officer in the background. The gunners lie prone at the feet of their kneeling loaders; all wear the new cylindrical soft hat with attached cloth star-and-crescent badges. Despite their inadequacies these captured weapons were immediately pressed into service by the hard-pressed Nationalist Army.

Berthier M1907/15 rifles and Mle 1892/16 carbines, were acquired for first-line troops. Second-line troops received a confusing variety of weapons, including the old French 11mm Gras M1874 which had been in Greek service before the Mannlicher-Schönauer; this rifle and its carbine version had been popular amongst various irregular forces in the Balkans since the turn of the century. Other rifles used by second-line units during the Asia Minor campaign included war-booty Bulgarian and Turkish models captured during the Balkan Wars. Large numbers of captured Turkish 0.45in Peabody-Martini M1874s were pressed into service, as well as 20,000 of the externally identical Martini-Henry Mk Is which had been purchased from Great Britain in 1886.

The light machine gun used by the Greek Army was the French M1915 CSRG ('Chauchat'), which had entered their service in 1917. Medium machine guns were mainly the French St Etienne M1907, but a batch of 160 US Colt M1914s (6.5mm versions of the M1895 'Potato Digger') were also used. During the early fighting in Asia Minor the Greeks also captured a number of German Maxim MG08 heavy machine guns from the Turks. Some of these were refurbished or repaired and put back into service with Greek rear units; 400 Austrian Schwarzlose guns were also used, some of them purchased and some captured in 1912–13. It was also reported that a number of French Hotchkiss M1914 medium MGs were ordered by mistake in 7.92mm calibre.

Turkish small arms

Two of the main semi-automatic pistols carried in the Ottoman Army in 1914–18 were the 9mm Parabellum version of the Mauser C96 and the FN-made Browning M1903. Most rifles in service with the Nationalists were also from pre-1918 Ottoman stocks. The four main models were the Mauser M1890, M1893 and M1903 rifles and the M1905 carbine, all in 7.65mm calibre. Other types in service included the Italian 6.5mm Mannlicher-Carcano M1891, either left behind by their retiring forces or sold later commercially. A number of 0.303in Lee Enfield rifles used by the Nationalists may have been captured during World War I from the British forces in Mesopotamia, but most came from the defeated Armenian Army which had been supplied by the British. (In January 1921 Mustafa Kemal sent an ironic message to British Prime Minister Lloyd George, thanking him for the 40,000 rifles received from this source.)

Old single-shot Peabody-Martini M1874 rifles were also used by the Nationalists, but had a distressing habit of refusing to fire more than five rounds before jamming; eventually the fault was rectified in Turkish workshops with a local adaptation. The shortage of small arms during the early phase of the war meant that all rifles and machine guns had to be kept in service whenever possible, and by 1921 there were hundreds of small workshops repairing damaged firearms and producing ammunition for the Nationalist Army.

The heavy machine guns used by the Nationalists appear to have been almost exclusively German Maxim MG08s. These came from several sources; ex-Ottoman Army weapons were used in the early fighting, but machine guns supplied by the Soviet Union after 1921 probably included war-booty MG08s captured by the Russians during 1914–17. There is little photographic evidence of any other types in service, and the only others seen in use were a handful of 0.303in Vickers Mk I guns. However, significant numbers of captured Greek 'Chauchat' LMGs were certainly pressed into service.

The Greek crew of an elderly British 6in howitzer prepare to fire towards Turkish positions in Asia Minor. The great majority of the Greek artillery had French equipment, but in 1917 the British Army had supplied 40 of these heavy pieces, dating from 1896, for use on the Macedonian front.

Sources of Nationalist weapons

The Nationalists' shortage of arms prompted a number of raids on depots in Allied-held Constantinople. In January 1920 one such raid on the Akbas arms depot captured 8,000 rifles, 40 machine guns and 20,000 cases of ammunition which had been stockpiled there to be sent to the White Russian armies fighting in the Russian Civil War. Another raid on an arms depot at Gallipoli gained the Nationalists 8,500 rifles, 33 machine guns and 500,000 cartridges. Underground Nationalist organizations in Constantinople also sent 1,500 rifles, 320 machine guns, 2,000 cases of ammunition and one heavy artillery piece. More significantly, they also sent 56,000 gun locks taken from Turkish rifles impounded by the Allies in 1918–19, which could be used in Nationalist workshops.

After the signing of a pact between the Soviets and the Nationalists in March 1921 the latter received 6,000 rifles, 5 million rounds of small-arms ammunition and 17,600 artillery shells. In 1921 the Greeks captured a number of Mosin-Nagant M1891s that were fresh from Soviet factories, but the Nationalists had also found old caches of arms left behind by the advancing Russian Imperial Army during its campaigns in the Caucasus in 1915–16. (How much use they were able to make of these weapons, which had been buried for up to six years, is not recorded.)

After 1921 the Italians and French sent large shipments of armaments

A Nationalist medium artillery piece photographed during the advance on the port of Smyrna in 1922. This is a German-supplied, ex-Ottoman Army 7.5cm Krupp *Feldkanone* M16 'New Type'. Note that the gunner peering round the shield wears the new 'peakless képi'.

Officers of a Greek communications unit are driven through an Anatolian town in a Ford Model-T car. Both officers wear a lighter shade of the M1908 uniform, contrasting with their driver's green-khaki woollen version.

A Greek Army transport mule loaded with the barrel section of a disassembled mountain gun during the advances through Western Anatolia in 1921. Much of the Greek artillery was equipped with mountain guns, and although the army had a significant number of motor vehicles they still relied heavily on draught animals for transport of all kinds. As the Greek supply lines lengthened they became more susceptible to attack by Turkish irregulars and regular cavalry.

to the Nationalists; when one Italian supplier was asked why he was selling weapons to his country's former enemy, he replied candidly 'because they pay'.

Greek and Turkish artillery

The Greek artillery employed in 1919–22 was mainly composed of French 75mm Schneider M19 mountain guns and 75mm M06 field guns. A number of 65mm Schneider-Ducrest M06 mountain guns had also been donated to the Greeks by the French late in World War I, and Schneider built 75mm M06/09 mountain guns designed by the Greek Col Danglis. The survivors of 144 75mm M1897 QF field guns used by the Greeks during the Balkan Wars were also pressed into service. Most of the heavier guns in use were elderly French 120mm De Bange M1878 and 155mm M1881/1912 pieces. The Greeks had been supplied with 40 British 6in M1896 howitzers in 1917, and used some of them in Asia Minor. They also obtained Czech 10.5cm and 15.5cm Skoda guns from Ottoman depots, but these were sent to Thrace to have their missing breechblocks replaced and did not see service.

Turkish Nationalist artillery during the war was largely equipped with ex-Ottoman Army field guns which were hidden from the Allies in 1918 or repaired by the Turks. Most of the latter had their removed breechblocks expertly reforged using scrap steel from locomotive wheels and other engine parts. Ex-Ottoman Army guns used included 7.5cm Austro-Hungarian Skoda M15, Krupp M05 and Rheinmetall M08 and M14 mountain guns. In the German 7.7cm calibre, field guns included the Krupp-Ehrhardt M96 and Rheinmetall M16, and there were also some 7.7cm Rheinmetall M15 mountain guns. Heavier mountain guns included the Austro-Hungarian 10cm Skoda M16 and M16/19, and the 10.5cm Krupp L/12. Other 10.5cm pieces employed by the Nationalists were the Austro-Hungarian M14/T field howitzer, the Krupp M98/09 and the Rheinmetall M16. There were only a handful of heavier 15cm guns in service, these being the Krupp L/12 and M1905 quick-firing howitzers.

In early 1921 the Nationalists had a total of 103 guns in service, but later they received artillery from the French and Italians and were reportedly supplied with large amounts of ammunition. One German observer noted that the Nationalists had also received from the Soviets many French-made field guns captured from the defeated White Russian armies. By mid-1922 they had more than 320 guns in service, enabling the formation of artillery units at infantry division level, and these were particularly effective during the battle of Dumlupinar. During that year Italian firms signed agreements to supply the Nationalists with large quantities of equipment, including eight batteries of field artillery, Fiat trucks and some aircraft.

(Continued on page 33)

GREEK ARMY, 1920–22
1: Private, Infantry, 7th Division, 1920
2: Corporal, 5/42nd Evzone Regt; 'Plastiras
   Detachment', 1922
3: Staff sergeant, Artillery, summer 1921
4: Lance-corporal, Cavalry Division, 1921

GREEK ARMY, 1921–22
1: MajGen Nikolaos Trikoupis, 1922
2: Colonel, Signal Corps, 1921
3: Standard-bearer, 33rd Inf Regt, 1921

B

GREEK ARMY, 1921
1: Sergeant, Gendarmerie; III Corps, Bursa
2: Able seaman, Greek Navy landing party
3: Circassian irregular

THE CALIPHATE ARMY, 1920
1: Corporal, *Kuva-Yi Inzibatiye*
2: Lieutenant, Sultan's Infantry Bodyguard
3: Circassian volunteer, *Kuva-Yi Ahmediye*

D

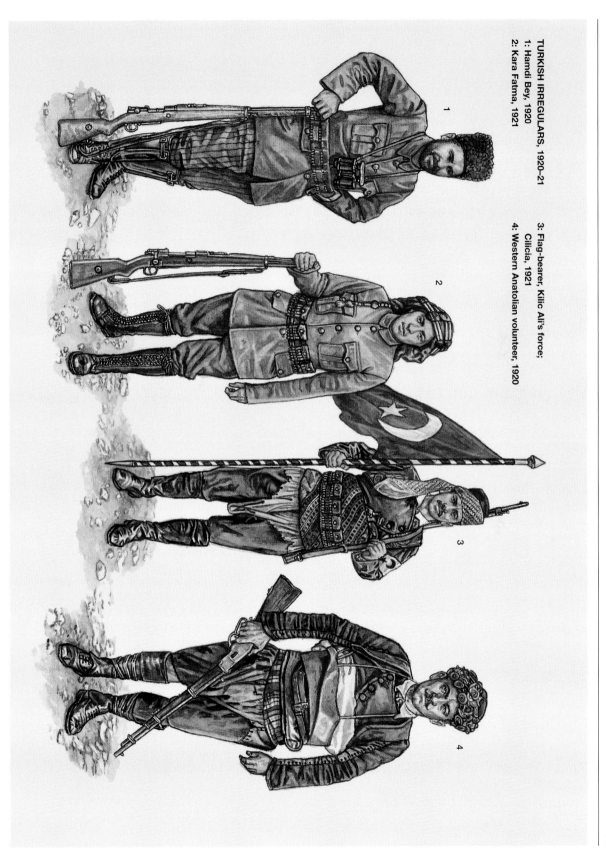

TURKISH IRREGULARS, 1920-21
1: Hamdi Bey, 1920
2: Kara Fatma, 1921

3: Flag-bearer, Kilic Ali's force;
   Cilicia, 1921
4: Western Anatolian volunteer, 1920

E

TURKISH NATIONALIST ARMY, 1921–22
1: Corporal, 14th Cav Div, summer 1922
2: Sergeant, Infantry, summer 1922
3: Private, Infantry; Eskisehir, 1921
4: Corporal, 1st Assault Bn; Sakarya river, August 1921

F

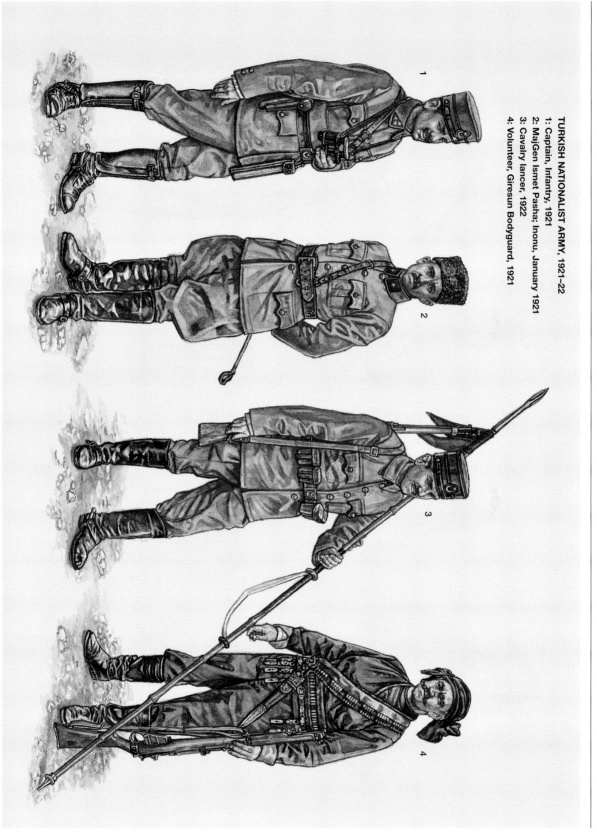

TURKISH NATIONALIST ARMY, 1921–22
1: Captain, Infantry, 1921
2: MajGen Ismet Pasha; Inonu, January 1921
3: Cavalry lancer, 1922
4: Volunteer, Giresun Bodyguard, 1921

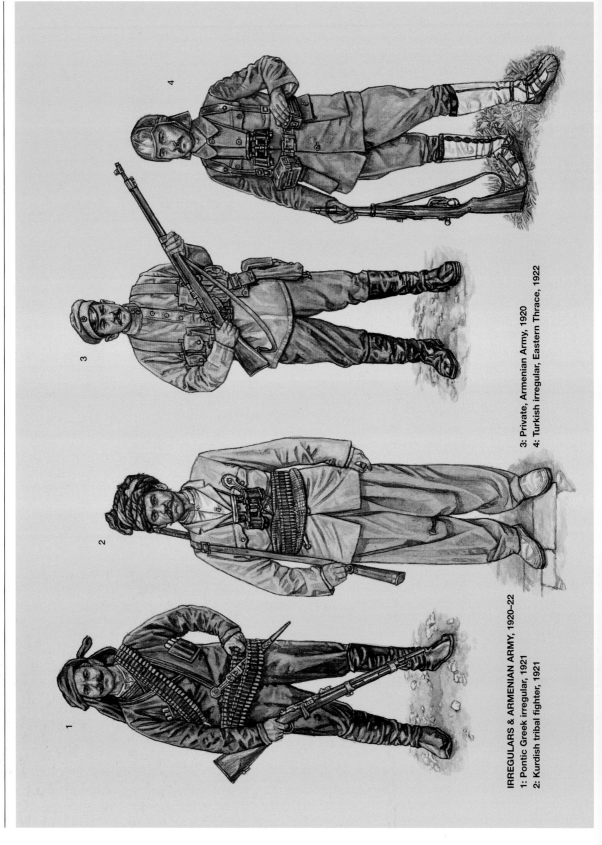

IRREGULARS & ARMENIAN ARMY, 1920–22
1: Pontic Greek irregular, 1921
2: Kurdish tribal fighter, 1921
3: Private, Armenian Army, 1920
4: Turkish irregular, Eastern Thrace, 1922

Two Greek soldiers of the Transportation Corps fasten a load to the back of a camel; these beasts were used by both sides during the war. The load in this case includes a chair and poles for an officer's tent along with a field chest to carry his uniforms and kit.

Military transport

The immense distances over which both armies operated during the war made military transport very important. The Greek Army Transportation Corps began the war with 900 trucks, 250 officers and 2,500 drivers. Their vehicles included 100 US-supplied Kissel trucks ordered by the Greek Army in 1914, Ford Model-T cars and patrol cars, and Fiat 1.5-tonne trucks. During the campaign in the near-desert conditions of Anatolia such vehicles often proved unreliable and had to be abandoned. Many of them had served previously on the Macedonian front in 1917–18, and were in a poor state before they even arrived in Asia Minor.

The Nationalist Army had very few motor vehicles at the start of the war apart from a handful of staff cars. From 1921 the Turks bought a number of trucks from the French and Italians, although the numbers reported in some sources are greatly exaggerated. Allegedly, some 400 were supplied by France and 1,500 by Italy before the Nationalist summer 1922 offensive, but in reality the total number of motor vehicles reported in service in August 1922 was 298. Draught animals were used by the Greeks to pull their artillery, and mules to carry mountain guns. Camels were also widely used by both sides to carry supplies and to transport some of their lighter artillery. The Greek Army requisitioned any available camels, horses, donkeys and oxen from the Anatolian population, which naturally increased their unpopularity. On the Nationalist side another important means of transporting supplies to the front was on the backs of female porters; at several crucial moments during the

Greek airmen with a French-supplied Breguet 14A2 reconnaissance bomber, one of the main types in Greek service in 1919–22. The aircrews are all wearing fur-collared French flying overalls with brown leather helmets. Although Greeks and Turks made up the great majority of pilots some foreign airmen are reported to have flown during the war; a Canadian claimed that he had flown for the Greeks, and a few Germans reportedly flew for the Nationalists. In general, the Greek forces attracted few foreign volunteers. Two English officer veterans of the Great War did sign up to fight in Asia Minor using false Greek names; one served in the artillery, the other at first in the machine gun corps and later in a signal unit.

The Turkish Nationalists' most famous pilot, Fazil Bey (centre, leather coat) stands in front of his Albatros D.III fighter, which bears a white numeral '1' on the white-edged black square national insignia. Like the army, the Nationalist air arm had to acquire its equipment from whatever sources it could, including captured aircraft and a few cannibalized leftovers from 1918.

war much-needed supplies were carried to the front lines by these women volunteers.

Armoured vehicles

There was little reported use of armoured vehicles by either side. The Greeks had purchased a few British Peerless armoured cars in the aftermath of World War I; they also tried to buy 25 to 30 French FT-17 light tanks, but the attempt was blocked by the French government. There are no reports of the Greeks receiving armoured vehicles from other sources, and they deployed no tanks in Asia Minor.

After the French reached an accommodation with the Nationalists in 1921 they left behind small arms and artillery when they withdrew from Cilicia, and reportedly handed over some FT-17s from their disbanding 5th Light Tank Battalion. In September 1922 the Nationalists were reported to have used seven of the FT-17s along with French 75mm guns during their capture of the city of Ushak.

Greek and Turkish air arms

The Greek air forces in Asia Minor were divided between the Army Air Force (HAFC) and Naval Air Service (HNAS). In total the HAFC had 70 aircraft, comprising mainly French SPAD S.VII, SPAD S.XIII and Nieuport 24 fighters and Breguet 14A2 reconnaissance bombers. Naval aircraft included British Airco DH.9 reconnaissance bombers and Sopwith Camel 1F.1 fighters. The Greeks are reported to have assigned 55 aircraft of all types to Asia Minor, in one Navy and four Army squadrons.

The Turkish Nationalists began the war with a handful of ex-Ottoman Air Force machines, which had often been repaired by cannibalizing other aircraft. These included single examples of German Rumpler C.IV, DFW C.V and AEG C.IV reconnaissance planes, and two Pfalz D.III fighters cobbled together out of four found in storage. Three ex-Ottoman Air Force Albatros D.IIIs were repaired in 1920, and one survived the war. Other aircraft used were a SAML/Aviatik B.1 bought in Italy, and ten Breguet 14B2s bought from the French. In 1922, 20 SPAD S.XIIIs were purchased with funds donated by Turks working in Germany. A Naval Flying Service was also formed, with four Gotha WD.13 seaplanes that had been smuggled out of storage in Constantinople.

The most important role of both air arms in 1919–22 was to carry out reconnaissance, although some bombing missions were also flown; the Greeks launched several raids by up to seven DH.9s on Kütahaya and Eskisehir in July 1921. The huge expanses over which the air arms operated meant that air-to-air encounters were rare; so far as is known, the total number of claimed air-to-air victories was a paltry three for the Greeks and one for the Turks.

UNIFORMS

THE GREEK ARMY

The Greek soldier went to war in 1919 wearing a modernized version of the M1908 green-khaki woollen uniform worn since the Balkan Wars of 1912–13 (see Plate A1); slight modifications had been made since 1913 and during World War I.[1] Although the woollen uniform is described as greenish-khaki its actual colour, as with those of other armies, varied depending upon the factory of origin. Officers wore green-khaki uniforms based on the M1908 model (see Plate B2) purchased from military outfitters. Their usual tunic had a closed stand-and-fall collar, pleated breast pockets with scalloped flaps and large patch pockets on the skirts with straight flaps, but, as was usual for the period, slight details of cut and quality depended on the taste and wealth of the individual. Officers wore breeches with riding boots or leather gaiters and ankle boots. Some staff officers are reported to have worn British khaki uniforms that retained their original 'lion and unicorn' General Service buttons.

Foreign-made uniforms were increasingly acquired as the Greek Army expanded, and these included ex-US Army jackets (see Plate B3); large numbers of US war surplus uniforms were disposed of in the Near East after World War I, some also being used by the Turkish, Georgian and Armenian armies. Reportedly the Greeks also ordered quantities of French horizon-blue uniforms in 1921. Canadian stores to the value of £2 million that were left behind in England were also sold to the Greeks in September 1919. In the chaotic situation in Asia Minor it is not known exactly to what extent US, French and Canadian surplus uniforms were worn by the Greek Army, as they are usually not easy to distinguish in monochrome photographs.

Headgear

The headgear in service included the M1908 soft-crowned field cap with a brown leather peak (visor), which came in slight variations of shape; officers wore a smarter képi version. Another widely worn type was the M1917 sidecap, which was modelled on the *bonnet de police* in use by the French Army since 1890. Both these caps had the same cloth badge on the front, with the royal crown in yellow or white (depending on branch of service) above a blue-white-blue national roundel. Both types of cap were worn in desert conditions with a sun curtain (see Plate A3).

The Greek Army wore French-supplied Adrian M1915-pattern steel helmets when available, and these came in several models. From 1917 some officers wore an official pattern with the Greek badge on the front; other ranks wore plain helmets without applied insignia (see Plate A4), many of the latter reportedly being French factory rejects which were

A smartly uniformed Greek officer (right) supervises the collection of captured Turkish rifles and swords, which are being loaded onto the back of a local porter; his men in the background wear a mixture of woollen sidecaps and an Adrian helmet. On his collar a buttoned tab in branch-of-service colour is visible, and on his left sleeve two gold inverted service chevrons.

1   See MAA 356, *Armies in the Balkans 1914–18,* and MAA 466, *Armies of the Balkan Wars 1912–13*

A Greek sergeant photographed relaxing while serving in Asia Minor in 1919. He wears standard M1908 green-khaki woollen uniform with the field cap. Note on his right sleeve the two diagonal stripes indicating his rank; these were in yellow or white depending upon the 'button colour' of the branch, on a broader backing of branch facing colour. His brown leather belt has four mounted-troops' ammunition pouches with central strap-and-button fasteners.

sold to the Greeks at a discount. Other examples seen in photographs have various indistinguishable crests on the front. Amongst the war booty captured by the Nationalists were Adrian helmets with the Royal Thai Army badge applied, presumably diverted to Greece from orders placed by Thailand from 1917 onwards. Some Greek soldiers photographed in 1921 appear to be wearing ex-Belgian helmets with the lion's-mask badge still affixed. Other Adrians may well have come from stocks left behind in Salonika after 1918 by various armies, including both Serbian and Imperial Russian troops.

Summer and winter clothing

The summer uniform worn by the Greek Army was a khaki drill version of the M1908 (see Plate A3); the lightweight khaki cotton often faded in the sun to a very pale shade. In the heat of the Asia Minor plains troops not surprisingly wore as little as possible; while there is no photographic evidence that shorts were ever worn, in the field most Greek soldiers would wear their undershirt along with either the winter wool trousers or the summer version if available. During the Anatolian winter the standard M1908 greatcoat was worn with the woollen uniform, and other overcoats in service also included ex-Canadian, British and US Army models. Greek officers wore both long and short models of double-breasted greatcoat. Some winter items like pullovers may have been supplied by the Entente powers from their surplus stores, and others would have been sent by the soldiers' families. As the first winter approached in 1919 the Greeks asked the British to supply them with 200,000 pairs of woollen socks but, as with other such requests, it is not known if they arrived in time to reach the front line.

Branch colours

The Greek Army's branch-of-service colours were as follows, displayed as pointed tabs on the tunic collars: red for the infantry, Evzones (elite

The crew of a Greek Army 75mm Schneider-Danglis M06/09 mountain gun photographed during the winter of 1921–22. Their greatcoats should be the Greek M1908 model, but these were running short by this date, and with the expansion of the army coats were purchased from British, Canadian and US sources.

mountain light infantry), and medical corps enlisted ranks only; dark green for cavalry; black for artillery; pink for engineers; dark blue for the gendarmerie; orange for the commissariat; chocolate-brown for artisans (carpenters, builders and other trades), and white for adjutants. Medical officers were identified by purple and veterinary corps officers by deep purple. Officers wore tabs on both tunic and greatcoat collars with an added 'branch-metal' button: gold for infantry, Evzones, artillery, paymasters and ordnance corps; silver for cavalry, gendarmerie and commissariat. Enlisted ranks of the gendarmerie also wore collar-tab buttons as a distinction of their special status.

Insignia of unit and rank

While they are seldom visible in photos of troops in the field, regimental numbers might be worn in several ways, including cloth Arabic numerals on the tunic shoulder straps and small metal numerals on the front left of the M1917 sidecap.

Non-commissioned ranks were identified by diagonal braid stripes on the lower sleeves of the tunic: lance-corporal, 1 narrow stripe; corporal, sergeant and staff sergeant, 1 to 3 broad stripes. The stripes were in 'button' colours: yellow for infantry, Evzones, artillery, paymaster and ordnance corps and aircrew; white for cavalry, gendarmerie, pioneers and commissariat, all backed with branch facing colour.

Officers' ranks were shown on the képi by a system of black cord bands: ensigns and sub-lieutenants, 1 cord; lieutenants, 2 cords; captains and majors, 3 cords; lieutenant-colonels, 4 cords; and colonels, 5 cords. All general officers had a broad black braid képi band and a gold chinstrap, and showed their exact ranks on their shoulder boards. Most ranks had gold crowns surmounting the cockade of the cap badge, but sub-lieutenants and lieutenant-colonels had silver crowns.

The rank insignia on officers' shoulder boards depended on the branch of service. For officers of infantry, Evzones, artillery, paymaster and ordnance corps and aircrew the insignia were: sub-lieutenant, lieutenant and captain, 1 gold lengthways stripe and 1 to 3 silver stars; major, lieutenant-colonel and colonel, 2 gold stripes and 1 to 3 silver stars. Officers of the cavalry, gendarmerie, pioneer and commissariat corps wore the same but in reversed 'metals'; e.g., a major of cavalry wore 2 silver braid stripes with 1 gold star. General officers had gold braid shoulder boards with 1 to 3 silver stars for major-generals, lieutenant-generals and full generals.

Other insignia

Chevrons worn points-up on the left upper sleeve were issued one for each period of six months' continuous front-line service; they were not issued to second-line personnel such as supply troops. Regarded as badges of honour, the chevrons were gold for officers and yellow for other ranks. Wound chevrons were worn on the right upper sleeve; for officers these were gold or silver depending on the branch of service, while other ranks wore plain black chevrons.

The only other field signs worn by the Greeks were icon-style pictures of King Constantine issued to pro-monarchist units, which were worn tucked into hat bands.

A Greek regular posing for a studio portrait before going off to Asia Minor in 1919, wearing a uniform in various shades of woollen material. His sidecap and puttees are in the standard green-khaki shade, as is the shirt collar folded outside the collar of his tunic. Both his tunic and breeches are in a darker and presumably heavier wool material. The belt equipment is puzzling: his ammunition pouches are not Greek issue, nor are they recognizably those of any other European army of the period.

Turkish irregulars photographed at Hatay near to the Syrian border during the early phase of the war, together with two civilians (top left and centre). The man at top right, presumably their commander, wears a *kalpak* and a tunic with triangular collar patches. The others wear Arab *kufiya* headdresses as was normal in the southern provinces (note that some of these are obscured by inked lettering on this photographic print). Clothing varies from a patterned traditional shirt to suits with collared shirts and ties. Multiple bandoliers are worn for the various Turkish Mausers, the weapon at centre left being an M1903 carbine; note that the same man seems to have a holstered, long-barrelled Luger artillery pistol.

Equipment

The Greek troops that landed at Smyrna in 1919 were almost totally equipped with M1908 leather equipment: a brown leather belt with three side-fastening, box-like 50-round ammunition pouches, worn flanking the buckle and centrally at the rear supported by Y-straps; a bayonet frog; a slung canvas haversack, a knapsack and, if they were lucky, a water bottle. Cavalry, horse artillery and other mounted troops wore different pouches fastened with a buttoning strap at centre front. When knapsacks were unavailable many soldiers carried their small kit and personal affects in a rolled groundsheet and/or blanket. As the war intensified many of the new reinforcements sent to Asia Minor were equipped from varied sources. These included items captured during the Balkan Wars from the Ottoman and Bulgarian armies; Serbian Army equipment left behind in Corfu when its remnants took refuge there in 1916; and items left behind by the British, French and other Allied forces stationed on the Macedonian front during World War I. Gas masks were issued to some Greek troops and gas drills took place during training, although there is no evidence that they were ever needed.

TURKISH UNIFORMS

Turkish irregulars

The irregular fighters of the *Kuva-Yi Milliye* in Anatolia from 1919 were mainly dressed in civilian clothing. Traditional costumes varied according to region and ethnicity – whether Turkish, Circassian, Arab, or from another group; it is impossible to describe an 'average' irregular fighter, and the reader is directed to the examples in the illustrations. Any available items of former Ottoman uniform would have been worn, and some irregulars presented a mixture of military and sometimes exotic civilian clothing. Veterans of the Ottoman Army would have returned from the front in 1918 with some elements of uniform and equipment, though the former would usually be too tattered to wear by 1919. Because many of the irregulars had often been fighting as bandits before 1918 they were usually well equipped with bandoliers. The only insignia seen in use by the irregulars were white armbands worn with civilian clothing (see Plate E3), bearing a sewn or stencilled red star-and-crescent.

Nationalist Army uniforms

As with all aspects of the Turkish Nationalist Army, the uniforms worn by the troops were 'begged, borrowed or stolen' from many sources. Troops began the war in 1920 wearing whatever M1909 Ottoman Army uniforms were available mixed with civilian clothing, but when the army surrendered in October 1918 many of its uniforms had already been reduced to rags. Very few Nationalist soldiers wore what could be described as a regulation uniform, and even in photographs of small groups wide variations are obvious. Old uniforms that were still in military stores were issued, and 10,000 were smuggled to Ankara from Constantinople. The simple design of the Ottoman Army uniform for the rank-and-file meant that it could be manufactured (or approximated) in local tailors' workshops following simple line-drawn patterns, since many tailors were illiterate. Such sources continued to produce basic uniforms, from whatever materials were available, during 1919–22. Footwear was always in short supply for this hard-marching army, and when leather boots were not available fabric peasant shoes were worn, although some Turkish troops reportedly went barefoot.

The pre-1918 khaki uniform tunic often had no breast pockets and many also lacked waist pockets; significant numbers of late-manufacture examples were not true tunics at all but of pullover design, with a placket to mid-chest. By 1922 a typical woollen tunic had a stand-and-fall collar and six front buttons, the latter sometimes concealed by a fly flap. Tunics might be made with or without shoulder straps, and with or without breast and/or waist pockets. Colour shades varied widely, and every type of available material was used. (Such was the shortage of materials that Mustafa Kemal even suggested that carpets should be cut up to make uniforms.) Breeches were usually woollen, also in a variety of khaki shades, and were normally worn with cheap and easily made puttees.

Officers usually wore pre-1918 uniforms or newly made versions of them when they could get them. Their M1909 uniform came in various shades, but grey-green was the most common, and this was worn with the lambswool *kalpak* or the new-style 'peakless képi' (see below). The old Ottoman branch-of-service colours displayed as officers' piping and collar facings and other ranks' collar patches had been: infantry, olive-green; machine-gun companies, grass-green; cavalry, light grey; artillery, dark blue; engineers, mid-blue; railway troops, sky-blue, and gendarmerie, scarlet. Officers' German-style (and often German-made) straight or interwoven braid shoulder boards had been backed or edged in branch colours, with ranks indicated by stars; Nationalist officers discarded shoulder boards and moved their rank to collar patches (see below, 'Nationalist rank insignia, 1920–22'). Legwear for officers was not standardized; from photographic evidence it appears that junior officers wore puttees or leather gaiters with ankle boots, and more senior ranks high riding boots.

An eyewitness account of the fighting in 1922 describes the wide variety of clothing worn by the Nationalist troops: 'There are picturesque Lazis from distant Eastern Provinces, garbed entirely in black. They have tight blouses, trousers with skin-tight pants and baggy seat, leather puttees and soft leather moccasins. Capping all a black turban is wound

These Turkish irregulars, including drummers, are taking part in a victory parade in the city of Marash in the southern province of Cilicia after withstanding a siege by French and Armenian forces in February 1920. They wear the usual mix of traditional and paramilitary clothing; some have scarves wrapped around either a red fez or a white cap. At left foreground, note what seem to be German 'disc' hand grenades attached to the belt. The flag is an old Ottoman standard, which was used by these men alongside improvised star-and-crescent banners.

tightly round the head. Ammunition belts encircle the waist and pass over both shoulders, loaded with cartridges for their modern Lebel rifles. They are further armed with a short poignard [dagger], and often with an ultra-modern German "potato masher" grenade. There are Arab troops from the Southern provinces – city dwellers, not nomads – in conventional olive drab or homespun, with stout boots and a "burnous" [kufiya] headscarf thrown over their heads. There are Kurds, many in grey civilian coats and breeches, black boots, with a gay kerchief tied over their heads. Most of them carry a knife as well as a rifle and a bayonet. All the Turkish troops are great fighters with cold steel'.

Nationalist headgear

During the early fighting against the Greek, French and Italian armies in 1919–21 the Nationalist Army continued to wear various qualities of the Ottoman Army's World War I *kabalak* or *'Enveryiye'* sun hat named after Enver Pasha, made of a strip of fabric wound in various ways around a wicker frame (see Plate D1). Roughly cylindrical soft woollen or cotton caps in white were also worn before 1921, sometimes bearing a printed black-on-white badge of a star above an upwards crescent.

From 1920 onwards a new type of brown or khaki cylindrical soft cap was seen in use, based on a slightly stiffened band with a hessian or stiff cotton crown of various heights (see Plates F1 & F2); this is sometimes termed a *kalpak* from its general shape, but for clarity in this text we reserve *kalpak* for the traditional lambswool hat. These caps came in many styles and colours due to their ad hoc manufacture; some were fairly compact, while others had the crown extended upwards to almost resemble the headgear worn by the Ottomans' historic janissary corps. On the front a simple red star-and-crescent badge was either stitched directly or attached on a sewn-on cloth backing.

Another new type of headgear was initially seen in use by officers from 1919, but also by many of the rank-and-file by 1922. This stiff 'peakless képi' style (see Plate G1, and studio photo on page 18), was based on the shape worn by seamen of the Ottoman Navy during World War I; the absence of a peak was significant to Muslims, so that nothing prevented their foreheads touching the ground during prayer. This cap also had a red star-and-crescent badge on the front, on a khaki or sometimes a green cloth backing. It continued to be worn alongside the cylindrical cloth cap late into the 1920s, and some photos show officers wearing it with a pair of motoring goggles.

Photographs show select Nationalist units wearing the Turkish steel helmet, which was an adaptation of the German M16 with the front brim cut back, and a few also show Nationalist troops parading in the original German M16. Neither type seems to have been worn to any great extent in the front line, as they had never been supplied to the Ottoman Army in significant numbers.

Four Turkish soldiers photographed wearing uniforms typical of the Nationalist Army by 1922. The tunics and breeches are made from light khaki cotton, and vary slightly in detail. What is presumably a junior or warrant officer (second from left) has dark collar-facing, box pleats on his tunic waist pockets, and leather gaiters instead of puttees. All four wear the dark lambswool *kalpak*, and the Ottoman Army belt with star-and-crescent buckle, though two also have waist bandoliers.

Festooned with bandoliers, these determined-looking Nationalist troops appear from their legwear to be cavalrymen. The officers in the front rank wear military tunics, and two of them brass star-and-crescent badges on the *kalpak*, while the men behind them have civilian clothing. The front-rank men have semi-automatic pistols tucked into their bandoliers, including at least one Luger P08, what appear to be an Italian Beretta M1915 and a Mauser C96 'broomhandle'. The rank rings worn around the cuffs (far right) are unexplained.

Foreign-made uniforms

The Nationalist Army also used a wide variety of foreign-made clothing. Eyewitnesses describe soldiers wearing French horizon-blue shirts and trousers; these may have been captured from the Greek Army or bought directly from the French. Large quantities of US Army surplus uniforms were reportedly bought from French sources after being left behind by the American Expeditionary Force (these were also used in significant numbers by post-war French Colonial troops). One eyewitness specifically mentions Nationalist troops wearing ex-US Army greatcoats. In June 1921 a force of up to 20,000 Nationalist troops was reported to have been wholly or partly issued with Italian uniforms left behind when Italian forces withdrew from their base at Antalya; eyewitnesses state that some Nationalist prisoners taken by the Greeks wore the Italian grey-green woollen tunic with Turkish rank insignia. Other uniforms reportedly even came from British stores in Constantinople, thanks to officers who were privately sympathetic to the Nationalist cause.

Cavalry uniforms

The Turkish cavalry had by 1922 developed into the elite of the Nationalist Army, and were issued with the best available uniforms and equipment. Most wore ex-Ottoman Army uniforms or new ones based on the old regulations. Nearly all equipment and weapons were pre-1918 Turkish, although there were reports of some Romanian sabres being given to the Nationalists by the Soviets. Several lancer regiments were in service by the end of the war, and one of these wore the peakless képi covered in black oilcloth with the star-and-crescent on the front (see Plate G3). Lances carried by these 'unofficial' lancers were ex-Ottoman pattern, but with black-over-red pennants instead of the previous plain red swallowtail. Other headgear worn by the cavalry included either the new cylindrical cloth hat or, more usually, the lambswool *kalpak*.

Western eyewitnesses were often impressed by the appearance of the Nationalist cavalry. One noted that a unit he saw were 'splendid men wearing new spotless uniforms and Circassian caps'; another described troopers uniformly equipped with three ammunition bandoliers each. In 1922 one of the first units to enter Smyrna was reported to have worn black uniforms with a black fez bearing a red star-and-crescent on the front.

Nationalist rank insignia, 1920–22

The former Ottoman Army ranking system for enlisted men featured transverse bars on shoulder straps in branch colours (e.g. yellow bars across green straps for infantry non-commissioned officers). When the Nationalist Army was formed in 1920 this system was discarded in favour of a new sequence, which was retained until 1924. Non-commissioned officers now wore their ranks on a green or khaki patch on the left upper sleeve of the tunic. Ranks were identified by red vertical stripes: 1 to 4 for corporals, sergeants, assistant sergeant-majors, and sergeant-majors respectively.

Ranks for second lieutenant to captain were worn on the tunic collar on a triangular green patch: 1 to 3 silver five-pointed stars, for second lieutenant, lieutenant and captain respectively. Field officers wore square green collar patches with 1 to 3 silver stars for major, lieutenant-colonel and colonel respectively, and general officers red patches with 1 to 3 gold five-pointed stars for major-general, lieutenant-general and full general. Officers' ranks were also indicated by a sequence of cords or braids around the base of the new 'peakless képi' cap: subalterns and captains wore 1, field ranks 2, and general ranks 3 cords.

Equipment

Most Nationalist Army equipment came initially from Ottoman Army M1909 stocks. By 1918 shortages had left relatively little in store, and there was a diversity of equipment available to different formations. Those serving in far-flung garrisons obviously suffered the greatest shortages, while those in garrisons near Constantinople were better equipped. Any former Ottoman Army units left in place after the Mudros Armistice were reduced in size in accordance with its terms, so would have been able to concentrate available stocks for issue to their remaining troops. Sympathizers in Constantinople also managed to smuggle 15,000 precious ex-Ottoman Army water bottles to the Nationalists. (Water bottles were always in short supply, and the Turks had to resort to using ordinary tins instead; reflections from their bright surface reportedly gave away Turkish positions on several occasions.)

Although there is little specific evidence, it would seem that the Nationalist Army must have acquired equipment from the French and Italian forces when both withdrew from Anatolia. They certainly left behind small arms, and it is logical that other surplus equipment would also have ended up in Turkish hands. Officers usually used whatever equipment they had left over from their Ottoman Army service, and other examples were acquired from friendly Italian, French and British officers.

Caliphate Army uniforms, 1920–22

The ineffectual Caliphate Army continued to use pre-1918 Ottoman Army uniforms and rank insignia. The majority of Caliphate soldiers continued to wear the *kabalak* (see Plate D1) in Constantinople until the Nationalist takeover in 1922. According to descriptions others wore the old-fashioned red or khaki fez, which some covered with scarves. Officers continued to wear their pre-1918 uniforms with the lambswool *kalpak* or the officers'-quality *Enveryiye*.

PLATE COMMENTARIES

A: GREEK ARMY, 1920–22

A1: Private, Infantry, 7th Division, 1920

This soldier wears the standard winter woollen uniform of the Greek Army, with the M1917 sidecap bearing the yellow-crowned national cockade of the infantry. On his greenish-khaki tunic he displays the plain red collar tabs of the infantry branch, and on his left sleeve four inverted yellow chevrons on red infantry backing show that he is a World War I veteran who has served four six-month periods of service in the front line (these did not have to be consecutive). His woollen trousers, puttees and brown boots were all standard issue to the first Greek troops sent to Asia Minor. Equipment is also standard M1908 issue, with Y-straps supporting on the belt the three ammunition pouches carrying 6.5mm clips for his Mannlicher-Schönauer M1903 rifle. He holds a spare magazine for the 6.5mm version of the French CSRG 'Chauchat' that was the standard Greek light machine gun.

A2: Corporal, 5/42nd Evzone Regiment; 'Plastiras Detachment', 1922

This corporal of the elite Evzones mountain light infantry carries a French-supplied 'Chauchat' LMG, and is armed for self-defence with a holstered Steyr M1905 semi-automatic pistol. The famous 'Plastiras Detachment', made up of this unit and a small artillery element, fought with some distinction to the very end of the war. The traditional Evzone uniform consists of a khaki fez or *farizan* (though the black tassel was usually removed in the field), and a *doulama* coat over a *fustinella* kilt and long, gartered woollen stockings. His rank of corporal is indicated by the yellow stripe on red backing on his coat sleeves. Although his pigskin *tsarouchia* mountain

shoes with black pompons might look impractical, they were sturdy and comfortable to wear.

A3: Staff sergeant, Artillery, summer 1921

From photographic evidence, this senior NCO's mixed summer uniform of M1908-pattern items is typical. The woollen field cap is from his winter uniform but has a sun curtain attached to shade his neck. The collar of his light khaki cotton summer tunic bears the black branch-of-service tabs of the artillery, and his three rank stripes are displayed on both forearms. The trousers are in winter-weight woollen material, and are worn with woollen puttees. Some Greek weaponry and equipment in 1919–22 came from French sources; this man has an 8mm Mle 1892 artillery carbine and leather equipment from stores left behind in Salonika in 1918.

A4: Lance-corporal, Cavalry Division, 1921

This senior soldier from the Cavalry Division wears the French Adrian M1915 steel helmet; like most of those supplied to the Greek Army in 1919–22 this is plain, with no applied frontal badge. The cavalry's dark green branch colour is shown on the tunic collar tabs, and this was one of the branches of service distinguished by a white cap-badge crown and rank insignia. On his right upper sleeve a single black inverted chevron shows that he has been wounded once. The fact that he does not have any white chevrons on his left upper sleeve means that as yet he has not completed a full six months' front-line service. His woollen breeches are worn with leather gaiters and ankle boots, although some Greek cavalry received riding boots. On his leather belt he has the ammunition pouches with central button-down flap straps that were particular to mounted troops. He is armed with a Mannlicher-Schönauer M1903/14 carbine, and a cavalry sabre.

B: GREEK ARMY, 1921–22

B1: Major-General Nikolaos Trikoupis, 1922

As commander of the Greek Army's I Corps this general was also given command of II Corps and a division from III Corps at the crisis of the battle of Dumlupinar on 28 August; five days later he was captured with some 5,300 of his men. (In captivity, he would be informed by Mustafa Kemal that he had been promoted to replace LtGen Hatzianestis as C-on-C of the Army of Asia Minor.) He is wearing the double-breasted short greatcoat that was a popular alternative to the more cumbersome long-skirted pattern for field use. His rank of major-general is displayed by a silver star on his gold braid shoulder boards and his status as a general officer on the collar as well as on the tunic collar underneath. His officers' képi has the general officers' gold chinstrap and patterned black band, with the gold crown and blue-white-blue cockade badge. Like most high-ranking officers the general will have purchased his uniform and leather equipment from the best military outfitters in Athens.

B2: Colonel, Signal Corps, 1921

On the officers' version of the modernized M1908 field

This trooper of the 300-strong Sultan's Mounted Guard belongs to one of the few military units that the beleaguered Turkish ruler could call upon in Constantinople. The guard were well mounted on black horses, and were usually seen in the capital in this light blue dress uniform – compare also with Plate D2.

uniform this colonel wears the plain blue collar tabs of the Signal Corps with a gold-coloured button. His shoulder boards are backed with branch-of-service blue, and bear the two lengthways gold braid stripes and three silver stars of his rank. Each of the gold inverted chevrons on his left upper sleeve indicates six months' front-line service. His rank is also shown on the band of his M1908 képi, by five black cords, and a gold-wire crown surmounts the cockade. His 'Sam Browne' belt supports a Steyr M1912 semi-automatic pistol.

B3: Standard-bearer, 33rd Infantry Regiment, 1921
This veteran sergeant serves in a unit of the 5th Division under II Corps, which was commanded by King Constantine's younger brother Prince Andrew. He is wearing the type of mixed uniform that became commonplace in the expanding Greek Army, with a red '33' on the shoulder straps. His summer-weight cotton field cap is worn with an ex-US Army olive drab tunic from surplus American Expeditionary Force stocks, bearing sergeant's rank stripes on the forearms in the yellow-on-red of the infantry and Evzones. His trousers and puttees are standard green-khaki woollen issue, worn with brown boots. Greek regimental flags did not carry any distinguishing numerals to identify the unit; in the centre of the field is the image of St George slaying the dragon, and the finial is a Greek Orthodox cross.

C: GREEK ARMY, 1921
C1: Sergeant, Gendarmerie; III Corps, Bursa
The Greek Gendarmerie were heavily involved in protecting their army's overextended supply lines in Asia Minor. This NCO wears the summer version of the distinctive

These parading Greek infantry wear the summer version of the 1908 uniform with Adrian M1915 helmets, and present arms with Mannlicher-Schönauer rifles.

During the expansion of 1921 most regiments seem to have acquired three battalions; by mid-1922 divisional establishment was 10,000–12,000 men in three infantry regiments plus an artillery unit with between 8 and 24 guns – the artillery was widely dispersed.

Gendarmerie uniform, with an M1917 sidecap. On his sleeves he has the double white braid stripes of his rank, and on his left shoulder the white cord aiguillette distinctive to his branch. His collar tabs and shoulder straps are in branch-of-service midnight blue, the former with silver-coloured buttons. His equipment is light but functional, featuring waist bandoliers. Water bottles were vital in the heat of the Anatolian summer, and this gendarme has been fortunate to receive an ex-British Army example. Rifles issued to the gendarmes were often either captured from the Turks or dated back to the Balkan Wars; in this case the sergeant has an ex-Bulgarian Army Mannlicher M1890 carbine captured in 1913.

C2: Able seaman, Greek Navy landing party
Sailors from the underemployed Greek fleet were used in significant numbers as second-line troops, protecting the Army's supply lines from Turkish irregular attacks. This sailor displays the Cyrillic cap tally of the Greek battleship *Kilkis*; his white summer jumper with the red rating chevron of able seaman is worn together with Army-issue trousers and puttees. Equipment and weaponry are also provided by the Army: M1908 leather gear, and a new Mannlicher-Schönauer M1903/14 rifle.

C3: Circassian irregular
Most of the Circassian irregulars who chose to serve alongside the Greek Army wore civilian clothing. The lambswool hat came in various styles and qualities depending on the individual. To distinguish him from Circassians fighting with the Nationalists this man has been issued with a plain white armband as a field sign; some of these may have borne some stencilled motif, but as a Muslim he would not have worn anything featuring the Greek Cross. His boots are made from soft leather, and he carries a whip to control his Anatolian pony; also in the fashion of the region, over his colourful sash he is swathed in bandoliers with clips for his ex-Ottoman Army Mauser M1890 rifle, and carries a long Caucasian ('Circassian') dagger.

D: THE CALIPHATE ARMY, 1920
D1: Corporal, *Kuva-Yi Inzibatiye*
This corporal belongs to the short-lived 'Disciplinary Force' that was raised in Constantinople in 1920 to fight against the Nationalists. The troops who served the sultan's government usually had pre-1918 Ottoman Army uniform, and this soldier wears a *kabalak* hat with his mud-khaki woollen tunic, breeches and puttees. His shoulder-strap rank, one yellow bar on green, is of the pre-1918 system, signifying the nominal continuity of rule of Sultan Mehmed VI in Constantinople. However, his kit is not all 1914–18 issue, and his civilian bandolier underlines the ad hoc nature of some of this force's equipment. The formation of the Disciplinary

Force was encouraged by the Allied powers, who supplied them with arms; his Mauser M1890 rifle has probably been re-issued from their stores of weapons taken from the defeated Ottoman Army.

D2: Lieutenant, Sultan's Infantry Bodyguard

During the Allied occupation of Constantinople these troops were one of the most visible signs that the sultan was still officially in power. This officer wears the dress uniform that was introduced during World War I; it was basically the same design for all ranks, although some senior officers wore white breeches with a red seam-stripe. Other ranks had a brass star-and-crescent badge on the *kalpak* hat, in place of this officers' type with the Ottoman coat of arms. Despite their gaudy appearance the bodyguard troops did not have a purely ceremonial role, as hinted by the lieutenant's Mauser C96 semi-automatic pistol. His sabre is the M1909 model for junior officers, slung from the officers' dress uniform belt.

D3: Circassian volunteer, *Kuva-Yi Ahmediye*

The traditionalist, pro-sultanate Circassian warlord Ahmet Anzavur raised his 'Army of Muhammed' in 1920 to fight the Nationalists. His followers, a mixture of Circassians and Abkhazians, were known for their merciless treatment of any captives unfortunate enough to fall into their hands. Anzavur's men wore civilian dress which depended on their ethnicity, but this volunteer displays the traditional Circassian costume worn by the majority of his followers. Although they are not visible here, he wears loose-fitting trousers with the blue Circassian coat, high-buttoned blouse, lambswool *kalpak* and soft leather boots. He is armed with a Mauser M1890 rifle and a Circassian sabre and dagger, and in the field would probably add more bandoliers – the cartridge-tubes on his chest are purely decorative.

E: TURKISH IRREGULARS, 1920–21

E1: Hamdi Bey, 1920

One of the prominent military leaders during the early period when much of the fighting against the Greek Army was done by Turkish irregulars, he displays a typical paramilitary outfit as worn by the more westernized of the Nationalist guerrilla commanders. A military-style jacket is coupled with civilian striped trousers, ex-Ottoman Army strapped gaiters and boots, and binoculars. A leather waist bandolier carries clips for his ex-Ottoman Army 7.65mm Mauser M1903 rifle; one photo shows him also armed with a Steyr semi-automatic pistol captured from a Greek officer.

E2: Kara Fatma, 1921

This famous female irregular leader was celebrated in Nationalist propaganda during and after the war. She wears the *kufiya* Arab headdress common in the southern and south-eastern provinces of Anatolia; sometimes she wore a civilian jacket, but on this occasion she has obtained a

military tunic and breeches that have been tailored to fit her slight frame, worn with leather field boots. Some photos show a Luger P08 pistol and a riding whip tucked into the top of her ammunition bandolier. Although she was known to use several types of rifle, she was most commonly seen with this Mauser M1905 carbine.

E3: Flag-bearer, Kilic Ali's force; Cilicia, 1921

Some Nationalist irregulars who fought the French and their Armenian allies in the southern provinces in 1920–21 wore a uniform of sorts. This flag-bearer is wearing traditional civilian clothing, with the addition of a white armband with the red star-and-crescent sewn to it; insignia were rarely worn by the irregulars, but more often by those fighting the French in the south. His flag is taken from a photograph; it does not appear to be a military type, but serves as his unit's standard. He is armed with a Lebel M1886/93 rifle captured from the French Colonial troops that made up a large part of the Cilician occupation force.

Demirci ('The Blacksmith') Mehmet Efe was a leader of the *Kuva-Yi Milliye* irregulars fighting against the Greeks early in the war; here he wears the traditional dress of his home region – compare with Plate E3. In December 1920 Col Rafet Bey, commanding the Southern Sector of the Nationalist Army's Western Front, arrested him after failing to persuade him to bring his several hundred horsemen under regular army command in the Afyon Karahisâr area. The useful men were absorbed into the army and the rest disbanded.

E4: Western Anatolian volunteer, 1920

The wide variety of traditional clothing worn by Nationalist irregulars meant that few volunteer bands looked exactly alike. This man wears a red fez covered with small floral rosettes, and his black bolero-style jacket is worn over a long-sleeved, double-breasted garment which fastens across his chest. The multiple scarves wrapped around the waist and his pantaloon-style trousers give him a rather exotic appearance, which may be deceptive. Many of the irregulars were tough brigands who had been playing cat-and-mouse with the Ottoman authorities for years, as is evidenced by this man's Winchester repeating rifle taken from a dead gendarme. Note the waist bandolier with a deep cover-flap.

F: TURKISH NATIONALIST ARMY, 1921–22

F1: Corporal, 14th Cavalry Division, V Cavalry Corps; summer offensive, 1922

This corporal wears a black lambswool *kalpak* hat with his smart greenish-khaki woollen tunic, and the black shirt worn

by some cavalry units. His breeches, riding boots and officers'-style 'Sam Browne' belt are all ex-Ottoman Army items. Nationalist cavalry were usually described as being well armed, and this man has been issued a Mauser C96 semi-automatic pistol as well as his heavy ex-Ottoman Army sabre; reportedly the latter was particularly feared by their Greek cavalry opponents, who did not have the same weight of sword.

F2: Sergeant, Infantry, summer offensive, 1922

Nationalist soldiers were often issued with uniforms, equipment and weaponry from a variety of sources. This NCO wears the cylindrical cloth hat based on those worn by Anatolian peasants, in this case with a star-and-crescent badge on an attached patch. Use by the Nationalists of French Army surplus horizon-blue cloth is described by many eyewitnesses. On his left upper sleeve note the patch with the two vertical red stripes of his rank of *cavus* according with the new post-1920 system. Although his trousers are ex-Ottoman Army issue his leggings and footwear are local peasant items. The locally made haversack and his bandolier are typical of the kind of basic equipment used by the hard-pressed Nationalist Army. Russian Mosin-Nagant M1891 rifles were gratefully received by the Nationalists after their pact with the Soviet Union in 1921.

F3: Private, Infantry, Eskisehir, 1921

This private also wears the new cylindrical hat, which was made locally from any available khaki or brown material and in varying heights. By 1921 this had largely replaced most pre-1918 headgear, as it was easy to mass-produce and gave the Nationalists a distinctive look. Badges varied slightly in design but always featured the crescent, and usually a star-and-crescent. His woollen jacket has also been manufactured in one of the workshops that sprang up in Nationalist-held territory; the rest of his uniform and equipment have been taken from Ottoman Army stores, including German-type ammunition pouches and (obscured here) a water bottle in its canvas cover. Although the Turkish Mauser M1890 rifle was not the most common type in service with the Nationalists, it did see widespread use in 1919–22.

F4: Corporal, 1st Assault Battalion; Sakarya river, August 1921

This soldier is a member of one of the elite 'stormtrooper' units formed from 1921 as spearhead elements in each Nationalist infantry division. Most assault troops appear to have been issued with steel helmets, usually the Ottoman Army model worn here, but this is the only visible sign of his status; no distinctive insignia were worn, and the rank stripe of *onbasi* on his left upper sleeve was common to all units. The rest of the uniform is made up of ex-Ottoman Army items, including his boots and the leather equipment with German-style pouches. Assault troops were always issued with the best available weaponry and equipment; in addition

A Pontic Greek volunteer to the gendarmerie stands guard in the town of Romkioi in 1922 during the closing stages of the war. He wears an issued gendarme's uniform complete with dark blue distinctions and white left shoulder cord, but retains his traditional *pashlik* black cloth headdress. His two bandoliers, each with a support strap, are typical of the region; but note the web leggings – possibly US Army surplus acquired by the Greek Army?

to his Mauser M1903 rifle this man carries grenades including two German-type 'potato-mashers'.

G: TURKISH NATIONALIST ARMY, 1921–22
G1: Captain, Infantry, 1921
This *yuzbasi* wears the new-style 'peakless képi' which was adopted by some Nationalist officers after 1920 alongside the *kalpak* and the pre-1918 *kabalak*, and which steadily replaced them. Captain's rank is shown by the three stars on the green triangular collar patches of his woollen tunic, but note the single green cord around the cap. As a member of Ismet Pasha's staff this officer has complete Ottoman Army equipment, including binoculars and a mapcase. The Turkish-model Luger P08 semi-automatic pistol was a popular sidearm with Nationalist officers.

G2: Major-General Ismet Pasha; first battle of Inonu, January 1921
Mirliva Ismet Pasha was one of the most prominent Turkish commanders of the war, and his decisive command of the Nationalist Army's Western Front in the defensive battles at Inonu in January and March 1921 was vital to the survival of Turkish resistance. He wears a very plain Ottoman Army officers' uniform with 'Sam Browne' belt, the only insignia being the major-general's collar ranking according to the new system introduced in about 1920.

G3: Cavalry lancer, 1922
During the latter stages of the fighting in Asia Minor a number of lancer units emerged 'unofficially' amongst the Nationalist cavalry. This trooper is wearing a greenish-khaki woollen tunic and breeches with high riding boots. His hat is a black oilskin version of the new peakless képi which may even be an ex-Navy item, and has a metal star-and-crescent badge. Other lancer units wore the new model of cylindrical cloth cap, or the older lambswool *kalpak.* The bamboo lance was an effective weapon in the open warfare of the summer 1922 campaign; he also has a slung Turkish Mauser M1903 rifle, and ex-Ottoman Army cavalry pouches on his pre-1918 belt.

G4: Volunteer, Giresun Bodyguard, 1921
This man is a member of Mustafa Kemal's tough bodyguard unit, which was made up of Topol Osman's Black Sea volunteers who had previously fought in a ruthless counter-insurgency role. The traditional all-black dress of the Black Sea coastal region served as their distinctive uniform, comprising a headscarf, light jacket, shirt, trousers and soft leather boots. Many Turkish irregulars from all regions wore the 'Circassian' belt and dagger, which came in differing designs. The ex-British Army 0.303in Lee Enfield rifle was used by the bodyguard alongside the more usual Turkish Mausers.

H: IRREGULARS & ARMENIAN ARMY, 1920–22
H1: Pontic Greek irregular, 1921
This fighter from the Black Sea region of Anatolia is fighting a guerrilla war against the Nationalist Army, and wears traditional all-black Pontic costume (compare with G4). The turban-style headdress or *pashlik* was worn in various ways according to individual preference; the light jacket was called a *kontesh*, the overshirt a *geleko*, and the tight-fitting trousers *zipkos.* The soft leather legwear comprises *meshte* gaiters over *tsapoulos* shoes. As with most irregular fighters during the 1919–22 war he carries several bandoliers of ammunition. Many Pontic *Palikare* fighters would already have had rifles, in this case an 11mm Gras M1874 carbine, but others were reportedly issued older Greek rifles and carbines from Army stores.

H2: Kurdish tribal fighter, 1921
This Kurdish irregular is from the Alevi tribe which rebelled against the Nationalist Army in 1921, but since many Kurds also fought with the Nationalists he could as easily illustrate the dress of their auxiliaries. His traditional Kurdish headgear is made up of a stiff woollen cap wrapped with a cloth to form a turban. He wears a cotton jacket over a long-sleeved white shirt, baggy *chroal* trousers and soft leather boots. His silk sash serves as a carry-all for his personal gear and also supports his traditional *khanjar* dagger. A typical bandolier carries rounds for his captured Turkish Mauser M1890.

H3: Private, Armenian Army, 1920
The Armenian Army that fought vainly against the Turkish Nationalists in 1920 was a large but poorly armed infantry force, with little artillery. This private belongs to one of the units that have been issued with a uniform, though many of his comrades wore civilian clothing. His headgear is a Russian-style peaked cap with an Armenian cockade (red, blue, orange centre), and he wears a Russian-style *gymnastiorka* field shirt, but with trousers and web gear from Canadian Army surplus stocks. Rifles came from a variety of sources; the Mosin-Nagant M1891 was the most commonly seen, but this Canadian Ross Mk III was also used.

H4: Turkish irregular, Eastern Thrace, 1922
While the main fighting went on in Asia Minor a 'sideshow' conflict took place in Thrace between the Greek occupying army and local Turkish guerrillas. The latter had a working arrangement with local Bulgarian nationalists, so there was some crossover of weapons and clothing. This guerrilla is wearing the brown leather helmet that was seen in use by many pro-Turkish Thracian irregulars. Although some commentators have confused this with the helmet of the Ottoman Fire Brigade in Istanbul, it is an item of headgear that was worn by various guerrillas in the region, including a version by Macedonian and Thracian fighters in the 1920s and 1930s. The rest of his clothing is a woollen jacket and breeches worn with typical Balkan white cloth leggings, and his footwear are locally produced *tsarvuli* shoes as used by several Balkan armies in the early 20th century. A Bulgarian leather belt and pouches carry ammunition for his Mannlicher M1895 carbine.

INDEX